Home Wine- and Beer-Making

Contents

Home Wine- and Beer-Making

H. E. Bravery

Hart-Davis, MacGibbon   London

Granada Publishing Limited
First published in Great Britain 1974 by
Hart-Davis, MacGibbon Ltd
Frogmore, St Albans, Hertfordshire AL2 2NF and
3 Upper James Street, London W1R 4BP

ISBN 0 246 10720 0
Printed in Great Britain by
Northumberland Press Limited,
Gateshead

List of Illustrations

Foreword

This book, like all of my others, is a fully detailed work; but whereas those told in words how to make wines, here I use pictures also, to show that wine-making is still a simple process by which anybody can make top-class wines for a very small outlay, and with the simplest of utensils. Easy to follow recipes and methods are included for all well-known home-made wines as well as many new recipes and simple methods for making wines with ingredients obtainable at your corner shop or supermarket.

It is well known that many home-made wines spoil upon keeping or 'somewhere' along the line of operations required in the making. In this book I will explain how and why this happens and show you how to prevent it, so that you are assured of first-class results.

Home-made wines today are indescribably better than those turned out some years ago. This is because we know so much about the subject now that we work to a set of foolproof recipes and methods which enable us to produce wines every bit as good, and often better, than many commercial products costing a pound a bottle or even more. Yet our wines need cost no more than 5p to 10p a bottle. Cloudy wines, bitter wines, acid wines, wines that turned to vinegar, tasted flat and lifeless or became thick and oily, are a thing of the past. We know what causes these troubles and we simply take the routine precautions to prevent them. All this is fully explained in these pages and you will be surprised how simple it all is, and what is more you will be simply amazed when you taste the quality of the wines you will make by following the simple recipes and methods given here. One of the delights of modern wine-making methods is that you do not have to wait several years for your wines to be worth drinking. They should be ready in less than six months from starting; indeed, some will be ready even sooner. There are others, made with certain fruits, which will need a year to reach their best.

This hobby has been booming in the past fifteen years in the same way as beer-making – fifteen years ago only two firms retailed yeasts and fermentation locks, and then only as a sideline. Today there are thousands of suppliers. They deal in every conceivable requirement of the amateur wine- and beer-maker and if you look around you will find one near to you as well as the list of suppliers listed at the end of this book. The picture is the same in Canada and USA. About twelve years ago I gave the necessary information to someone in Canada who wanted to be the first in the field of suppliers of wine- and beer-making materials there. Today he has branches (franchises) all over Canada as well as in almost every state in America. And there are many others in competition with him. If the results of modern wine-making were not top class all these suppliers would have been out of business almost before they began – the reverse is the case, with a new branch opening up in one town or another every week.

The old concept of home wine- and beer-making is as dead as the Mammoth. It used to be a bothersome task entailing the use of giant tubs and huge jars, with the fermenting wines hanging about the place for months on end. Today it is a simple, trouble-free process where the utensils are quite small and uncumbersome, where you can start off a two- or three-gallon batch and have it out of your way in less than an hour. And what is more, it can be ready for drinking in a couple of months.

Popular ingredients such as elderberries, blackberries and other fruits are still used, but today we also use tinned fruits from supermarkets, dried fruits, concentrated grape juices, dried herbs and heaven knows how many sorts and types of ingredients that ten years ago no one would have thought of.

So there it is. If you have been disappointed in the past, here you will find the reason and the remedy. Those just starting out will be delighted with the results – I can assure you of that.

Part One

Home
Wine-Making

One

Introduction

Despite the fact that a great deal has been written about wine-making in recent years, this book is an absolute necessity. I say this because although I have written many wine-making books, all of which have become best-sellers of their kind, and hundreds of articles on wine-making for such magazines as *Do It Yourself, Practical Householder, Home-maker, Popular Gardening, The Gardener's Chronicle, The Amateur Enologist* (in Canada), as well as many others, I have it on authority that there are still hundreds of thousands of people wondering what wine-making is all about. They are jogging along with out-of-date recipes, methods and utensils and with practically no idea of what they are doing except that they are following a recipe. This book not only explains what wine-making is all about in words, but it shows in pictures how all the simple processes are carried out.

Wine- and beer-making must be two of the most popular hobbies today. This is understandable, for the very simple reason that home-made wines, like home-made cakes and jams, are far better than most of those that can be bought in any shop or supermarket. I, and you too, can make a couple of gallons of wine in an hour or less. In three or four months, the wine is ready for use and you can be assured that provided you have chosen a recipe that will make the sort of wine you will like, you will certainly be delighted with it.

Wine-making today is not a hit-and-miss hobby where you are left wondering what the wine will be like. It is no longer a joke of a pastime. And there is no need to offer apologetically a 'little drop of something I made myself' to friends and relatives. You can offer it with the sure knowledge that your friends will not believe you made the wine yourself – unless they are already experienced wine-makers who will know at once that you have made a good job of it.

3

While on holiday a few weeks ago, I visited two horti-
cultural shows where they had a small wine competition.
And how sadly I sighed for many of the competitors – some
of the wines looked really well turned out, but others were
cloudy, some had deposits of yeast in the bottles, whilst,
heaven forbid, some had begun to ferment again owing to the
warmth of the show hall. There is absolutely no need for this
sort of thing today and I thought to myself, if only these
competitors had known a little more about wine-making every
bottle would have been brilliant, there would have been no
yeast deposit in the bottles and most certainly the wines would
never have started to ferment again. It is an undeniable fact –
one that I have to press home as often as possible – that wine-
making is a simple, trouble-free hobby where the rewards are
far greater than from most other pastimes. I often wish I could
get everyone interested in wine-making into one large hall
and to talk to them for hours about it, explaining why they
have the troubles they do and how they can be avoided. But
the best I can do is to write my books and hope that readers
will apply their common sense when using recipes and
methods.

All the reasons for wines being spoiled and how to prevent
this are discussed fully in later pages so that you are assured of
success. If your previous attempts have not been up to expectations, you will find here the reason so that next time they
will turn out just as you had hoped.

This book not only explains in simple non-technical lan-
guage how to make top quality wines, but it also shows you
how wine is made – perhaps a better way of putting it is to
say: how wine makes itself, once you have prepared the
ingredients.

One of the most important points to bear in mind is that if
you have been using different methods from those here – and
surely you must have been – do not say to yourself when reading directions as so many people do: 'Oh, this doesn't sound
quite right, so I won't do it.' Or, 'Surely this cannot be all that
important.' Or, 'Mother made wines, but I'm sure she never
did this.' And so you don't do it. This is just where thousands
of people go wrong. The methods here are easy to follow and
it is important that they be followed carefully. And even more

important is that if you want to succeed, read and understand all the factual information this book contains before you start to make the wines. If you do this you will be like the driver of a car or the pilot of an aircraft. You will know how to drive or pilot and you will know so much about the working of the engines and other parts that you will know instantly if something it not going according to plan. This book shows how all parts of the process of wine-making work, how each different process is interrelated, and how all form part of the process as a whole. So understanding the subject is just as important as following a recipe and method carefully. This book will give you a thorough understanding of the subject.

Two

Utensils

For Beginners

Whether you use a lot of utensils or not is a matter of choice. Some people collect so many items that one would think they had started a commercial winery. Yet all that is needed to start you off in this wonderful hobby is a two-gallon polythene pail as near white as can be obtained, a couple of one-gallon fermentation jars, a funnel about four inches wide at the top, two fermentation locks and the siphoning arrangement. Whether you need a corking gadget depends on the type of cork you choose to use. You will also need three or four pieces of butter muslin about two feet square for straining purposes. Almost all other items will already be in the house. These will be a colander – often useful for supporting the straining cloth and a mincer (if you decide to use one) and of course a large saucepan or two.

It is always best to obtain utensils from suppliers of wine-making ingredients and utensils, because they deal in non-toxic plastic whereas if you buy from hardware stores utensils may not be made of the correct material: some plastics are unsuitable – even dangerous – when put to our uses. (See list of suppliers at the end of this book.)

On no account use old stone crocks – once favourites for fermenting wines. These are often lead glazed and can therefore be dangerous by giving lead into the wines. Indeed, if you have anything that was used for wine-making many years ago it would be wise to rid yourself of the lot and start again with just a few items shown here. You will then be on the safe side.

Saucepans used for heating fruits or for boiling water and sugar syrup should be of good quality aluminium, monel metal, stainless steel or good quality enamel. If enamel, it

6

Fig 1

must not be chipped, otherwise the iron showing through will not only discolour the wine, but spoil the flavour and perhaps give metallic hazes into the wines.

Because most beginners will be making one-gallon lots for the first year or so at least, the above is all they are likely to need by way of utensils except that they will add a few more one-gallon jars for storage purposes and a few more fermentation locks so that their wine-making may be a continuous process instead of having to wait for the jars to empty and the fermentation locks to become available. Many will perhaps use two or three fermentation pails so that they have several lots fermenting at the same time.

For Experienced Wine-Makers

The utensils listed for beginners are quite suitable because
most want to get the feel of things with small amounts of
wine to start with. When they are experienced and realise what
wonderful wines they can turn out they will want to make
larger amounts. The utensils shown in this chapter will be
more in their line. The amount of wine you decide to make
each time will depend on how much you can use.

Fig. 2

Two great advantages come from making large amounts:
one is that wines made in large quantities, say three gallons
or more, are usually much better in quality than those made
in small lots. Another is that when you make large bulk lots
you can use some sooner than perhaps you ought to so as to
have some wine to drink while the rest is maturing in order to
become really first class. If making, say, three-gallon lots, two
gallons can be put away for a year or more while the one
gallon is your standby. If you do this with each three-gallon

lot started off at, say, six-weekly intervals you will have wine to use, and also be able to build up a really worthwhile stock. Then, later on, when some of your wines are three or four years old and really at their best, you can use them and replenish your cellar with new wine.

The benefits of using a fermentation vessel fitted with a heater and thermostat combined is fully explained in the section on making wines in a flat.

Three

What Sort of Wine Shall I Make?

Sweet or Dry?

We can decide at the outset whether to make sweet or dry wines merely by regulating the amounts of sugar we add. Normally two and a half pounds of sugar in one gallon of must will produce the maximum alcohol. Therefore if only this amount is used the yeast will use all of it to produce alcohol, leaving a bone-dry wine with no unfermented sugar at all. If, therefore, we want a medium sweet or sweet wine, we must add enough sugar to make the amount of alcohol as well as a little extra to be left unfermented to sweeten. All this is taken care of in the recipes so there is no need to work it out for yourself. When formulating the recipes, I have worked on the principle of pleasing the average palate, calculating that 'so much' unfermented sugar will make a medium dry wine to suit the average palate, and then tried to assess the amount to make a sweet wine that will please the average person. This is not quite so easy as it may sound for the simple reason that what amounts to a dry wine to some people is much too dry for others. Exactly the same applies to medium sweet, medium dry or the fully sweet wines. Only yourself, after having made two or three lots of wine, will be able to decide whether to use more or less sugar. But on the whole, if you use the recipes as they are you will be delighted with the results.

Body and Bouquet

The best way that I can describe body in wines is to call it

10

their fullness. A good example of this is found for example if you will taste a light dry wine and then a good quality port or sherry. The port or sherry, compared with the light dry wine, will have a fullness and robustness that we would not want in the lighter, drier sorts.

The production of body and bouquet in commercial wines of quality is produced automatically because of the sugar being natural grape sugar. But in most of our wines we add cane sugar which is used by the yeast to make alcohol for sweetening, but this sugar adds hardly anything to the wine itself. Natural grape sugar imparts bouquet to the wine, but much of the bouquet of certain commercial wines is produced by moulds which are allowed to collect on the grapes before they are pressed. The flavour of some commercial wines is also produced in this way. Sauternes and sherry are notable examples. Sherry with its characteristic flavour and bouquet cannot be made anywhere. This is because the flavour is imparted by what is called a 'flor'. How this is encouraged by the sherry producers of Spain to settle upon the wine to be turned into sherry is their secret. We know that it is done by exposing the wine to the air for long periods. Most attempts to make sherry by this means in this country will almost always result in the wine being soured by wild yeasts or bacteria or being turned outright into vinegar. I am sure that most of the cheaper sherries are not sherries at all but are made with a blend of ingredients that will produce an imitation in flavour, but not bouquet.

We can produce body and some bouquet quite naturally when making our wines whether we add anything to them or not. This is because the fruits used will produce a certain amount. But if we want more body we can add such things as raisins, which will add a vinousness (or vinosity) as well, or sultanas, or bananas. Bouquet comes naturally to a certain extent, and most wine-makers find this sufficient, but if you want a more pronounced bouquet, additional material will have to be added to produce this. You have only to savour the bouquet of flower wines to realise that a few flowers added to a fermenting must would produce additional bouquet. Having experimented with this sort of thing on numerous occasions, I am able to conclude that rose petals with a pleasing scent are

best for this purpose. Elderflowers, lime flowers and hawthorn
blossom may be used in small quantities, but to do this sort
of thing indiscriminately would not be sensible because the
bouquet produced might be quite foreign to the wine itself.
Imagine coffee which smelled slightly of tea. I make these
points so that experienced wine-makers can find their own
medium for making wines with additional bouquet.

Alcohol content, long storage and sensible handling of the
wine will help to produce bouquet. Having mentioned raisins,
sultanas and bananas as a means of obtaining extra body and
bouquet I must mention that I have included these in the
recipes where I feel that they will be most beneficial to the
wine. But this does not mean you cannot use them in some
of the other recipes if you want to. If you do this sort of thing,
always bear in mind that dried fruits as we generally know
them, dates, figs, raisins and sultanas, contain approximately
fifty per cent sugar. One pound of raisins for example contains
approximately half a pound of sugar. Therefore if you use
these dried fruits where they are not included in the
recipes you will have to adjust the amount of sugar recommended accordingly. Raisins will give flavour into the
wine, so will figs, but dates and sultanas will not. Dates might
if used in large quantities. It is important therefore to know
the flavour of the wine you are to make and then decide
whether another flavour incorporated into it would spoil it –
raisins might in many cases, and sultanas could be substi-
tuted.

Bananas will add body. These must be ripe but not black
or mushy. One pound of fresh bananas contains roughly five
ounces of sugar. If you buy bananas and intend to use one
pound in your wine you will need to buy one and a half
pounds because the skins from one pound of skinned bananas
weigh eight ounces. Some people chop up the skins as well
and use them but I do not like this.

Dried fruits should always be chopped finely or minced
before adding to the must. Bananas should be skinned and
then mashed and brought to the boil slowly (one pound of
bananas to a quart of water). Simmer them for about twenty
minutes and do use a saucepan twice as large as would
normally be needed as the liquid rises a great deal on boiling.

When using water as with bananas take this into account when calculating the overall amount to use.

This information is for your interest and if you are not yet experienced it would be advisable to stick to the recipes. Later, when you are more sure of yourself you can try out your own ideas.

Sweetening Finished Wines

It very often happens – especially with beginners – that they make some dry wine and then realise that they do not like really dry wine and what they should have made was a medium-dry sort. This is not the calamity many might imagine because it is quite easy to sweeten the finished product. This will not start off the second fermentation if the maximum alcohol has been made or if you have used enough sugar to make say thirteen per cent by volume. But if you began with less than two and a half pounds of sugar per gallon there is a risk that a secondary fermentation might be started if the conditions were suited to it – if, for example, the wine is kept in the warm. So if you decide to sweeten as shown here it would be wise to preserve the wine at the same time (see sections on preserving and fortifying, page 44).

The first thing to do is decide how much too dry the wine is before attempting sweetening. Normally, one teaspoonful of sugar will sweeten a wine that is bone dry to suit the average palate. Always use a little less sugar than you think you will need, otherwise you might over-sweeten and this is a problem not so easily remedied. For this reason it is best to sweeten one bottle to see how things work out. Put about one-third of the bottle into a china, glass or polythene jug and add one teaspoonful of sugar. Stand the jug in a saucepan of water over gentle heat and stir the wine constantly to dissolve the sugar without heating the wine too much. When all the sugar is dissolved, mix the treated wine with the remainder and sample it. If this is not quite sweet enough, you will have to repeat the process. When you know how much sugar gives the result you are looking for you can sweeten in bulk lots of a gallon with confidence if you want to. Do not forget to preserve your sweetened wine.

Four

The Cause of Wine Spoilage and How to Prevent It

If you follow the recipes and methods in this book and at the same time carry out the various recommendations for sterilising utensils etc., your wines will not be spoilt in any way. But it is still important that you understand why and how wines *can* be spoiled so that you do not become careless or disregard some instruction that might seem trivial and therefore unimportant to you. Indeed, when you have read about how wines can be spoiled you will at first wonder how on earth we are able to make wines successfully at all. But we do, and we do it so well that many people are almost dumbfounded at at being able to turn out such first-class products.

The main causes of wines being spoiled are floating about in the air, in the form of wild yeasts and bacteria. These are almost certainly on the fruits we use and on other ingredients. They are often to be found on corks, inside bottles, as well as on practically everything else we can use when making wines and beers. But we can destroy them easily as a matter of routine during the various processes, so that they don't have a chance of spoiling our wines and beers. But if we do not destroy them – if you disregard what may appear to you to be a trivial instruction – calamity will strike. And when this happens, wines and beers may turn to vinegar, turn sour, become flat and lifeless, become cloudy and over-acid upon storing, turn thick and oily or be spoiled and undrinkable for some other reason.

It is a lamentable fact that many people are still using

14

methods which call for crushing the fruits, adding water and allowing the wine to make itself by the yeast and bacteria on the fruits. Such methods were used in our grandmother's day with the result that more wines were spoiled than were any good at all. And those that did turn out fairly well could not hold a candle to the wines we make today.

As mentioned, when making wines by the modern methods in this book, all wild yeasts and bacteria are destroyed during the process of preparing the ingredients either by heat as in the Heat Treatment Method detailed in chapter 9, or by the sulphite solution prepared from Campden fruit preserving tablets as detailed in the Sulphiting Method in chapter 10. Therefore we begin our wine-making with a must (prepared mixture), completely free of the causes of spoilage.

But because wild yeasts and bacteria are ever present in the air, waiting to alight on anything on which they can live and breed, it stands to reason that we must protect our wines during the first operation until they are safely bottled and sealed as finished products. Fortunately all this is very simple. When the must is fermenting in a polythene bucket, it is best to cover the vessel with a sheet of polythene with no holes in it and to tie this down tightly with thin strong string. If the pail has a handle it would be best to remove it so that it does not prevent tying down the material to effect a close fit.

Alternatively you can use a special fermentation vessel with a closely-fitting lid. Either way, the gas generated during fermentation keeps up a constant outgoing stream to prevent the ingress of wild yeasts and bacteria. This also keeps at bay a tiny off-white fly which has been named wrongly the vinegar fly. You may never see one, but they are about and if they come into contact with the wine, the bacteria they carry will convert the alcohol in the fermenting must into acetic acid which is the main constituent of vinegar. This of course will give your wine the flavour of vinegar and there is nothing you can do once this has happened. The fly is often attracted into the house or winery by the pleasant odour of fermenting wine, so if you see one kill it at once.

Wines covered as advised are quite safe during the relatively short period of fermentation in the pail while the ferment is vigorous and the gas generated is sufficient to keep up a constant outgoing stream. But later, fermentation slows down with the result that production of gas diminishes, and when this happens the causes of spoilage could gain access. So, as will be seen in the methods, when fermentation begins to slow down, we transfer the wine to a jar and fit a fermentation lock (see illustration on page 30). This gives absolute protection against the causes of spoilage. When we carry out this simple routine we are assured of success. But if we put wines into unsterilised jars or bottles and use unsterilised corks the chances are that the wines would be ruined. So the precautionary routine must be continued, and the best means of doing this is to make up a sterilising solution as follows.

Sterilising Solution

Dissolve completely 2 oz. of sodium metabisulphite (obtainable from any chemists) in about a pint of warm water, put this into a half-gallon jar and fill to the shoulders with cold water. Such a solution will last for many months according to how often it is used.

The whole idea of preparing this is to have on hand the means of sterilising utensils quickly and easily whenever they may be needed. The solution must always be tightly corked.

When the time comes for wine to be put into jars or bottles, about one pint of this should be put into a jar, the jar should then be rotated so that all inside surfaces are wetted. The solution may then be put into the next jar which is treated in the same way. The solution should then be returned to the bulk for future use. Bottles are treated similarly but about half a pint of solution is enough for these. Using a funnel I can treat a dozen bottles in five minutes. Bottles and jars should be allowed to drain upside down for a few minutes before wine is put in them. A useful bottle rack can be made for this purpose (see Fig. 3).

Cleansing Dirty Jars and Bottles

During fermentation in jars, froth often collects under the

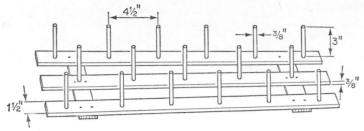

Fig. 3

shoulder and it does not necessarily remain part of the wine. It often forms a crusty deposit which cannot be reached with a bottle brush. Such deposits, as well as tannin stains, can be removed in minutes. Put about a dessertspoonful of bleach, such as Brobat, into the jar and fill to the brim with water. Thoroughly wash out several times with water when the deposit has floated off the jar.

The best way to keep bottles clean is to rinse them out several times with water when you have used all the wine and to let them drain upside down for a while. Leaving them standing with the dregs of wine in them will cause hard deposits to form as well as moulds which can only be detrimental in any winery.

Bottling

When bottling time comes along a simple routine should be practised. Firstly, if corks are hard, they should be put into hot water with something heavy on top to keep them submerged. About twenty minutes is enough. While these are soaking, bottles should be examined and if at all dirty, cleaned thoroughly with a bottle brush. They should then be sterilised as already explained. The corks should then be taken from the water, dried with a clean cloth and then immersed in some of the sterilising solution while the wine is being siphoned into the bottles. The corks may then be wiped on a clean cloth and inserted into the bottles.

Type of Cork

Flat-topped
mushroom shaped

Straight sided.
Requires to be
fitted with
corking gadget

Fig. 4

I always use the flanged-top mushroom-shaped cork because it can be pushed in by hand and removed without a cork-screw which means that they can be used and re-used as required if restored by the method on the next page. If this sort of cork is used, the bottles should be finished off with a plastic seal. These are supplied in a solution which keeps them expanded. When they are slipped over the tops of bottles they dry out to form a perfect airtight seal. Bottles closed like this may be stored upright. Where straight-sided corks are used a corking machine is needed and the bottles must be stored on their sides so that the wine is in constant contact with the cork to keep it moist – if it dries out, shrinkage would occur and wild yeast and bacteria as well as too much air would reach the wine and spoil it. Bottles fitted with straight corks may be finished off with tin-foil caps, but these are not satisfactory for the flanged-topped corks because they do not form a perfect airtight seal.

Corks and bungs often become mis-shapen during use so that they do not necessarily fit well when required for re-use. To restore them to their original shape, put them in warm water and bring it to near boiling. Oh, I know all the arguments about ruining corks when doing this. But I do it and have not yet ruined a cork or bung. Actually, I keep a little aluminium steamer for this as it collects the steam to expand the corks admirably without having to resort to trying to keep them submerged as would be necessary if a saucepan is used.

Fig. 5

Corks and bungs should be smooth, near white and not too porous. Buying them by the dozen is allowing yourself to be robbed; you can buy them by the gross for a quarter of the price (see Appendix for suppliers).

Siphoning

Siphoning is a simple operation whereby all the clear wine in a jar is drawn off without any of the yeast deposit being allowed to come over into the bottles. A siphoning pump is useful here, but I have always used a simple and inexpensive glass tube attached to a clear polythene tube to which is fitted a small tap. The whole arrangement need cost no more than twenty-five pence.

To make the siphoning arrangement: the glass tube with the end turned up is fitted to the clear polythene tubing by keeping one end of the polythene tubing immersed in very hot water for a minute or two. This end is then pushed on to the straight end of the glass tube. This can be used as it is merely by resting the upturned end on the bottom of the jar at the inside edge. The jar should be on a higher level than the tops of the bottles to be filled, as shown in the illustration (page 22). The other end of the tube is sucked until the wine reaches your lips. This is then pinched tightly, lowered into the first bottle and the wine allowed to flow. As the wine reaches just inside the neck of the bottle pinch to stop the

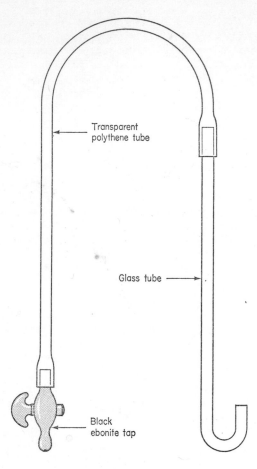

Fig. 6

flow slowly so that when the wine reaches two-thirds up the neck the flow can be stopped immediately. The tube is then held fast and lowered into the next bottle and so on until the last bottle is to be filled when the jar can be gently tilted towards the upturned end of the glass tube to allow all the wine to be drawn off. Small taps are available which can be

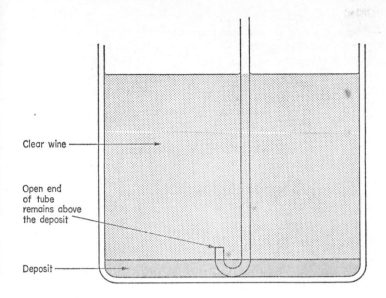

Clear wine

Open end
of tube
remains above
the deposit

Deposit

Fig. 7

fitted to the other end of the tube in the same way as the glass
tube – that is by heating the polythene tube so that it expands
easily for the tap to be pressed into place. These taps are
useful because you can turn off the flow as required. Indeed,
some of the tubing is so stiff of texture that it is difficult to
pinch it sufficiently to stop the flow. With this sort of tubing
a tap is therefore essential. Sterilising the siphoning arrangement is important. I merely pass a little of the sterilising
solution through this and then clear it with a little cooled
boiled water. I then wipe the whole of the outside with a piece
of cotton wool dipped in the solution.

Water

Readers of my earlier books will be familiar with the fact that
I always advocate boiling all water used in making wines.

Editors of certain magazines and other writers on the subject stress that this is not necessary, claiming quite honestly that our water supplies are quite safe. I agree that they are safe for human consumption, but there is always bacteria present, as well as the possibility of wild yeast. And it is for this reason that I advocate boiling all water. This report from the *Sun* dated 4 January 1973 might silence my critics, because clearly the bacteria in the water might well harm the wine:

'The Government should check Britain's tapwater for safety, the Consumer's Assocation says today.

Although the water is fit to drink, many places have a high enough bacterial or metal contamination level to warrant regular doom watch, the Association says in its magazine, *Which?*

It adds that bacteria levels are well below the safety limits set by the World Health Organisation.'

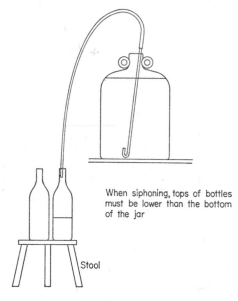

When siphoning, tops of bottles must be lower than the bottom of the jar

Stool

Fig. 7(a)

Five

Fermentation

Fermentation is the process by which alcohol is produced by the yeast, which in turn makes the wines for us.

In the section which explained how wines are spoiled I pointed out that we destroy the yeast on fruits and other ingredients and at the same time destroy wild yeasts and bacteria also present. This is done at the very beginning of making the wine. We are therefore left with a sterile product. This will not ferment and become wine unless we add yeast. True, if we left it uncovered for a day or so, wild yeasts, bacteria, the spores of moulds or fungi would soon alight on this prepared mixture to start a souring ferment. But we do not let this happen. As soon as we have prepared our mixtures for wine-making (musts, as they are called) we add a good yeast to make the wine for us. And, as we have seen, we keep the fermenting wines covered closely.

Now, when yeast is added as shown in the methods following, almost at once it begins to breed. But first, it converts the household sugar (cane sugar) to two simpler sugars so that it can live upon these in order to sustain itself. Being a living thing, yeast needs a reasonably balanced diet. This it finds in a well-prepared must containing organic matter from the ingredients, as well as tannin, acid and sugar. All these essentials are found in the musts we prepare in reasonably balanced proportions. And so the yeast begins to breed and multiply at such fantastic speed that millions of new yeast cells are produced in a matter of hours. This process goes on until what is called the maximum alcohol tolerance of the yeast is reached. When this happens, the yeast itself is destroyed by alcoholic poisoning so that no more alcohol is made. You will now understand why, when you add perhaps a teaspoonful of yeast you have perhaps as much as a pint or more after about ten days' fermentation. The expression 'alcohol tolerance' may sound somewhat technical. All it means is the amount of alcohol the yeast can tolerate; in other words the amount it can live in. Usually the amount is between fourteen and sixteen per cent by volume.

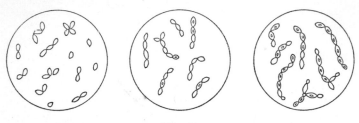

Fig. 8

Until this amount is reached the yeast continues to breed; millions of new yeasts are 'born', grow up and die in the process. When the maximum alcohol is attained fermentation ceases, no more alcohol can be made and no matter how long you may keep your wines they will not become any stronger.

But alcohol production is not all that takes place during fermentation. Indeed, the whole character of the must or liquid is changed. Flavours are changed also, esters and aromas are produced as well as bouquet. Esters which help to produce aroma and bouquet rely upon acids present in the must. Acids give the wine bite and freshness, tannin gives just the right amount of astringency, while the sugar forms the main requirement of the yeast. During fermentation it converts roughly half the sugar into alcohol and half into carbon dioxide gas which is seen as bubbles rising and passing into the atmosphere. During the early stages of fermentation frothing is seen and a hissing noise is quite audible. Indeed, it is so vigorous that when fruit pulps are fermented, the skins and pips rise up with the rising gas to form a 'cake' upon the surface. This must be pressed down daily and the fermenting must covered again at once. These directions are included in the methods so that you will not forget them.

Assisting Fermentation

Constant warmth during fermentation will help you to make wines ten times better all round than you can hope to make where the fermenting must is warm during the day and cool to cold at night time. Indeed, fermentation under these conditions is often far from satisfactory. One of the main problems when these conditions exist is that when, say, between ten to twelve per cent of alcohol by volume has been made, the yeast ceases to ferment owing to cold. The result of this is that a wine that should be bone dry is medium sweet, wine that should be medium sweet is sweet and what should have been a pleasantly sweet wine is much too sweet to be palatable. The simplest way of avoiding this is to keep the wine at a constant temperature of roughly 70°F. if you possibly can. (See section on Fermentation Cupboard, page 29.)

Where central heating is installed, there is no problem. Similarly, if you have storage heaters installed again there is no problem. The reason the wine trade does not have to resort to this is that they ferment for a short time until they have the wine they want and then arrest fermentation either by adding alcohol or by chemical means. But those of us who want the maximum alcohol in most wines cannot do this.

Another trouble when fermentation ceases before the maximum alcohol has been made is that when the wine is put into store the cold of the storage area usually prevents renewed fermentation until the warmth of spring or summer reaches the wine. When this happens the yeast becomes active again with the result that the wine becomes cloudy owing to the yeast rising with the renewed upsurge of gas and the corks or bungs blow out leaving the wine exposed to all the causes of spoilage. If this happens and you know about it in time to prevent spoilage bring the jar into the warm, fit a fermentation lock and leave in the warm until renewed fermentation has ceased. If the wine is in bottles, pour the lot into a jar and deal with it in the same way. This may be a nuisance, but you will obtain a much better wine for your trouble.

Another means of assisting fermentation is to use what are

called yeast nutrients. These are merely blends of chemicals designed to make good the deficiencies often found in our musts prepared from garden and hedgerow fruits and those made from ingredients other than grapes. You will see that whereas we use grapes which are fermented without the addition of water, we dilute our fruits and the juices they contain quite drastically by using only a few pounds to a gallon of water. We have to do this because most English garden and wild fruits are so high in acid and so astringent that if we used the juices undiluted the wines would be quite unpalatable. More sugar added to mask this would only produce an over-sweet wine, over-acid and too astringent to be drinkable. So we add nutrients to make good deficiencies that exist and these in turn assist fermentation to a satisfactory conclusion. But do not, just because fermentation is seen to be slowing down, add more nutrient. Add more than prescribed and you will spoil the flavour of the wine. In any case, interfering with wine during fermentation is one of the best ways to stop it prematurely. So once you have put the fermenting wine under locks as shown in the methods, do leave it alone.

The vigorous fermentation seen in the early stages cannot go on for long. Usually after about ten days it begins to slow down. At this stage or perhaps a couple of days either side depending on the methods, the still-fermenting wine is put into jars where fermentation will continue under fermentation locks for perhaps seven or eight more weeks. During this time fermentation will gradually become slower and slower until it finally stops altogether. And if you start worrying and go poking about with teaspoonfuls of yeast or nutrient tablets or some other additive or with an idea someone have given you, you will most likely stop fermentation when, if left alone, it would have continued until it ceased naturally owing to the maximum alcohol being reached.

Do not rack (take the wine off the deposit) during this stage. The methods in this book are designed to rid the yeast of most of the fruit particles or particles of other ingredients early in the process and therefore before the wines are put into jars. Some deposit will build up, of course, because the yeast is still multiplying, but there will be very little in the way of fruit particles – and it is these, being left in the wine for long periods, that often cause 'off' flavours. These flavours are difficult to describe, but they are the effect of decaying vegetable matter or fruit particles. But by all means rack when the wine has finally finished fermenting.

When Fermentation has Ceased

How can you be sure when fermentation has ceased? This is a question I have to answer very frequently and it is not an easy one. Those using the hydrometer (see page 38) can be certain when fermentation has ceased, but others will need to be observant. Experience is the thing and you can only obtain this by making many wines often and by watching their progress. This does not mean sitting beside the stuff all day for weeks on end, but it does mean taking a look at the ferment-ation lock once or twice a week – you will most likely do this anyway out of curiosity. When the wine is first put into a jar, fermentation may stop or slow down so much that bubbles do not pass through the solution for several hours afterwards. Put the wine into a cold jar and you will stop fermentation perhaps for good – especially if a goodly proportion of the maximum alcohol obtainable has been produced prior to this, so do warm the jars. My habit is to sterilise them and then warm them by rinsing under *hot* water, ensuring that no water ends up inside them. This protects the wine – or rather the yeast in it – from the sudden shock of cold. Norm-ally, though, fermentation will be on the go again within a few hours. This will most likely be quite vigorous with bubbles passing through quite rapidly – depending on whether you can keep the wine really warm or not. As fermentation slows the bubbles pass through less frequently so that after a few weeks one or perhaps two bubbles are seen to pass through in an hour. Later, it will be seen that the solution in the lock is pushed up on the out-going side and nothing appears to be happening. Leave it thus, or if you want to make sure that a little fermentation is still going on, give the jar a twist and you will see that a bubble or two will pass through the lock after a minute or two. So long as this state exists, leave the wine in the warm. Later you will see that the solution in the lock has returned to normal in the U-bend. This is the evidence that fermentation has ceased for good, but even then, it is still wise to leave it in the warm for one more week provided you do not need the space for more jars.

It is a fact that well-made wines will be clear to near brilliance at this stage. This combined with the fact that the solution has returned to normal in the U-bend is evidence that fermentation has ceased. Some wines will still be cloudy at this stage so you will have to rely on the solution in the U-bend in this event.

When you are satisfied that fermentation has ceased it is wise to take the wine off the deposit by siphoning it into other jars. This often presents a problem, especially if you are making one-gallon lots as most people do in the early stages of wine-making. The problem is that having siphoned the wine off the deposit, the jar of clear or near-clear wine is not full – and it should be if you propose to keep it in jars for any length of time. But if you propose to bottle it after say, three or four weeks this fact need not worry you. Simply bung the jar tightly and put it in a cool place until you want to bottle it. But if you propose to keep the wine in jars for several months, they really should be full because a large airspace over the wine can lead to spoilage.

Fortunately, I always have plenty of similar wines for topping up the jars, but this is not the case with those new to wine-making. So if you have no similar wine to fill the jars with, it would be wise to fill a half-gallon jar and to bottle the remainder. Some improvement in the wine will take place after this and despite the fact that such wines may not mature as well as they might, newcomers to the hobby will be quite content with the results. This little problem shows how wise it is to have plenty of wines of different varieties and you can only have this by regularly making them. Alternatively, double or treble all ingredients in the recipes and make two- or three-gallon lots. You may then keep one or two gallon in jars to mature thoroughly while some may be bottled for use as required.

Fermentation Cupboard

The greatest asset any wine-maker can have is a fermentation cupboard, unless you are using thermostatically controlled fermentation vessels as shown in the illustration of utensils for experienced wine-makers.

A fermentation cupboard can be made from the bottom of an old kitchen cabinet, wardrobe, or any other cupboard of similar size. Even a wall recess in a spare bedroom can have doors fitted and a small 100w. black heater installed quite cheaply. (These are supplied with a thermostat set at 70°F. and cost about £1.75.) If you fix yourself up with a cupboard like this you will never regret it, I can assure you. A good idea if you do this is to line it with polystyrene sheeting of the type sold at household stores for lining walls before papering. This will retain and reflect the heat and speed fermentation very greatly so that your wines are ready far sooner than they would be otherwise.

Such a cupboard can be converted to hold say three shelves to take six to nine one-gallon jars each or six two-gallon jars each. The heater should be placed on the bottom and the thermostat hung about two-thirds of the way up. The shelving should be made of strong timber of the sort used in airing cupboards, spaced in the same way to allow for warmth to circulate throughout. When installing shelving, do bear in mind that a one-gallon jar of wine weighs as much as twelve pounds or thereabouts – so do make sure that the shelving is secure.

Another means of keeping fermenting wines warm in jars is to use a heated tray. Electra Fibre Line, The Green, Rampton, Retford, Norfolk, market a shallow heated tray with the element completely encapsulated to make it a hundred per cent safe if wine is spilled into it. This holds five one-gallon jars and keeps the wine at the required temperature even if the room temperature is very low such as when wine is fermented in a shed. The tray is rigid and immensely strong.

Fermentation Lock

This is one of the most important parts of a wine-maker's armoury against wild yeast and bacteria already discussed in the section on wine spoilage. It not only keeps wild yeasts and bacteria at bay, but serves a most useful purpose in allowing you to judge the rate and state of fermentation. This fact has been emphasised in the section on fermentation.

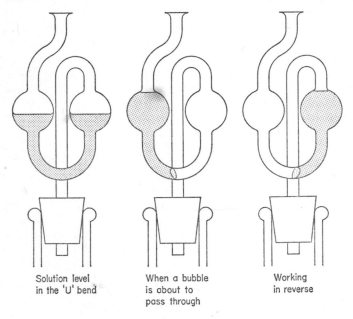

Solution level   When a bubble   Working
in the 'U' bend   is about to   in reverse
                      pass through

Fig. 9

As will be seen in the methods, during the early stages of production our fermenting wines are kept for a few days in a closely-covered polythene pail so that the gas produced during fermentation escapes through the puckers of the tied-down material and so keeps up a constant outgoing stream to keep the causes of spoilage from gaining access. But after a while fermentation slows down so that the amount of gas diminishes. And when this happens, the amount of gas being produced might not be enough to form a protective barrier. So at the appropriate time we transfer the wine to jars and fit a fermentation lock which ensures the safety of the wines during this secondary and somewhat slower fermentation period. The lock should be fitted as shown here. Always allow a quarter inch of the tube to protrude through the cork. This is advised because during use the lock and bung become very tightly united. Twisting the lock to remove it nearly always results in a broken lock and often a cut finger.

But with that quarter inch protruding, you can, while keeping the lock dead upright, place the end on a wooden surface and exert great pressure on the bung with the thumbs,

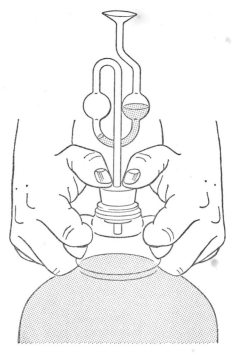

Fig. 10

if necessary, to remove it. Rubber bungs are notorious for tightening and the best way to remove these is to soak them in water for a minute or two and then treat them as above.

Having fitted the lock as shown, some of the sterilising solution is poured in to the level shown. During fermentation the gas formed escapes in a series of bubbles. These will be seen passing through quite rapidly for the first few days, but as fermentation slows down, so the rate of the bubbles passing through slows down also. If you watch you will see that the solution is closed up all the time (even whilst a bubble is passing through) to prevent air and the diseases it carries from gaining access. Apart from this important aspect there is the fact that this cuts off the oxygen supply to the yeast. Yeast must have oxygen during the fermentation period and if it cannot obtain it from the atmosphere as it would if the lock were not fitted, it turns to the sugar to manufacture oxygen for itself. In doing this it converts just a little bit more of the sugar to alcohol, which is important. As has been discussed in the section on fermentation, when all fermentation has ceased the lock is removed and the wine put away.

When the time comes for removing the lock, do so carefully. Rubber bungs take an almighty grip on the jars and I find it best to work these away from the edge of the jar with the thumbs, moving all round the jar as I do so. When it begins to loose its grip go very carefully otherwise is might come away suddenly. If this happens there is risk of some of the solution being drawn back into the wine. Cork will stick a bit and then come away without warning, so go carefully. One means of avoiding a lot of bother when removing locks is to ensure that you use bungs of a size that when pressed home as far as possible, protrude at least roughly five-eighths of an inch above the rim of the jar. Always be sure to press the bung with lock fitted down as far as it will go. Cork-made bungs go in easily, but it is wise to moisten rubber bungs so that they slip in with ease.

If a lock removed is not pressed into service immediately, remove the bung, wash the lock thoroughly in warm water, shake out the water and keep the lock where it cannot collect dust.

If during fermentation – as sometimes happens owing to an

unexpectedly vigorous ferment – froth passes into the lock, do not panic: leave everything well alone until the froth subsides. Then remove the lock, clean it and return it to the jar.

Choice of Yeast

It is sensible to try a variety of yeasts before settling for one particular sort sold under a brand name. Liquid yeast cultures are the purest and very often give better all-round results than the other sort known as general-purpose or multi-purpose yeasts. Obviously you cannot hope to know which gives the best results until you have tried several. Beginners are often foxed into using inferior yeasts believing them to be pure wine yeast, so do buy yours from a reputable dealer. I do not like recommending any particular yeast because while one sort might give me excellent results another operator might not have the same results and wonder what I found in that particular brand to recommend it.

There are a wide range of yeasts sold: for example, Burgundy yeast, Beaujolais, Tokay, Sherry and so on. But do not imagine that these will impart any noticeable flavour to any given must. Even a sherry yeast will not make your wine into sherry. Therefore, I advise you to use a good general-purpose yeast to start with and then try the liquid cultures.

Obviously the choice of most beginners with no wine in store and anxious to make a useful amount quickly will be for a vigorous yeast that will, when combined with constant warmth, make wine quickly for him. Tokay is a variety that will ferment at lower temperatures more satisfactorily than some others, but this will not necessarily ferment rapidly. So it boils down to using a reliable all-purpose wine yeast to start with and then trying others if you feel you might obtain better results.

One of the main factors in a satisfactory fermentation is the use of fresh yeast. For this reason it is not wise though it is often cheaper to buy larger than average quantities. This is sensible when you are making large amounts calling for a lot of yeast, but if you are making one-gallon lots at say monthly intervals your yeast can quickly become stale. Even those bought as fresh are often quite stale and if they are badly so, then fermentation, the rate of this, and the wine itself will suffer. It is useless to ask the assistant in the shop whether it is fresh or not. He will tell you that it is even if it has been on the shelf for years. One means of deciding whether a dried yeast is fresh or not is to open the carton. If the assistant complains call the manager and tell him that if you cannot inspect it you don't want it. A dried yeast should be very pale fawn in colour, completely dry and free of lumps. Always keep your yeast in a dry atmosphere avoiding extremes of temperature and once you have bought your supply use it up quickly.

Most suppliers will keep their yeasts in a place ideal for storing them but others put them in the window where the heat of the sun can only spoil them.

Acid and Tannin

These are important constituents of both the must and the finished wines. Without them the must would not ferment satisfactorily and the wine would lack freshness or 'bite'. If you analyse the underlying flavours of any wine you can detect the acidity as a pleasant tang upon the tongue while the tannin gives a pleasant and slight astringency noticed mainly when the wine is swallowed rather than when it is in the mouth. If you chew wine, roll it round the mouth and then swallow it slowly you will enjoy these flavours if only vaguely. But if they were not there you would notice their lack rather more than their presence because the wine would taste quite lifeless. Indeed, once you had swallowed it it would be gone; there would be no sensations in the mouth or throat to tell you that you had in fact tasted wine at all. In all the recipes in this book sufficient acid is given into the wine. This is not noticeable in recipes for fruit wines because fruits contain sufficient without the need to add any. But where flowers, vegetables and dried fruits are being used citric acid is recommended for the simple reason that these ingredients do not contain any.

I am often criticised for recommending this acid. It is agreed that citric acid is foreign to fruits other than citrus fruits – oranges, lemons etc., but the fact remains that yeast likes this acid and ferments extremely well in its presence. And I cannot find fault with wines balanced with citric acid. It is agreed that a blend of malic acid and citric is good, but not as good as some people would have me believe.

I am always conservative in the amounts of acid I recommend. This is because while, as we have seen, acid is necessary in a must for the purpose of a satisfactory fermentation and in wine for the purpose of rounding it off or balancing it, it is a very simple matter to recommend more than is to the liking of the average palate. It is far easier to add more acid than it is to remove an excess of it. If you use the amounts I recommend and then sample the wine during the later stages of fermentation when the wine is near brilliant you will know at once if a little more acid would benefit the flavour. If more is needed, add just a couple of crystals at a time, stir and sample again. Citric acid dissolves at once so there is no problem of dissolving it. By adding a few crystals at a time you may gradually increase the acid content without creating a situation where the wine becomes so acid that it makes you wince. The five millilitre spoon mentioned in the recipes for measuring the acid is the 5 ml. spoon issued with medical prescriptions.

Tannin

It will be seen in the recipes that I recommend a pint of strong tea. This is a cheap and readily available source of tannin and I cannot understand why some knowledgeable winemakers have a little giggle over my recommending it. Perhaps because grape tannin is the 'in thing' they think my recommendation somewhat old fashioned. If you prefer to use grape tannin by all means do so, but I find that tea gives equally good results and is always at hand. Four to five good-sized teaspoonfuls (there being many sizes and all are called teaspoons) to just over a pint of water is about right. Make the tea in the ordinary way, let it stand for ten minutes and then strain it into the must at the time given in the methods.

Clarifying

Every writer on this subject will tell you that well-made wines will clear themselves if given time. But they, cagey as most of us are, do not say what the term 'given time' amounts to. To the beginner this might mean anything from six months to ten years if a wine happened to take that long to clear. And this of course is most unsatisfactory. Now the fact is that well-made wines should be almost brilliant by the time fermentation has ceased. And when I say mine always are, I really mean always. Indeed, some are actually as brilliant as if they had been filtered and no matter how long I might keep them, those that are brilliant when fermentation ceases never throw a further deposit. Those that happen to be a bit hazy when fermentation stops always clear to brilliant a few weeks after racking. And that is just as it should be. I am sure that users of the recipes and methods in this book will be able to claim the same and prove for themselves that I am right.

Obviously it is helpful to know what causes persistent hazes or worst, heavy clouding, that will not settle out to leave a brilliant wine. Older methods calling for heating the fruits in order to destroy wild yeasts and bacteria on them, caused pectin to be boiled into the must and therefore into the wine. Pectin is a glutinous substance which holds minute solids in suspension to form permanent cloudiness. When I wrote my first book on this subject sixteen years ago, I recommended straining out through a jelly bag all pectin-bearing particles of fruit before heating them, and this worked well. But this was before pectin-destroying enzymes became available for general use by amateurs. Now we add them as a matter of course when heating juices so that they break down the pectin to allow the solids to settle out. The chore of straining through a jelly bag is therefore unnecessary.

Starch from ingredients such as potatoes, wheat, etc., acts in a similar manner to pectin.

Lack of tannin, insufficient acid, over-boiling of ingredients and metal contamination will also cause cloudiness, similarly an overlong pulp ferment as when fermenting the skins and pip of fruits.

However, readers will not have a clearing problem if they follow the recipes and methods carefully and use suitable utensils.

It will be seen that in the heat treatment methods I recommend Pectinol in the recipes. This will destroy the pectin boiled into the must so that the wine clears. In the sulphiting method heating does not take place so a pectin-destroying enzyme is not necessary. But if you add the boiled water before it has cooled, you could release some of the pectin in the fruits. However, and although, there is not likely to be pectin to hold solids in suspension in wines made by the sulphiting method it will do no harm to add Pectinol to ensure rapid clearing as fermentation ceases. Instructions as to when to add this are included in the methods.

The two enzymes mentioned in this book – Fungal Amylase for destroying starch and Pectinol for destroying pectin – are comparatively new preparations, though doubtless they will be better known by the time this book reaches the public. Certain starch- and pectin-destroying enzymes under proprietory names have been available for some time and although I cannot hope to have tried every one – mainly because I do not create a situation where their need arises in my ordinary wine-making – where I have done so I find them excellent.

Six

Using the
Hydrometer

Whether you use the hydrometer or not is entirely your own affair. I used to use it far more than I do now, but when I did use it I found it most helpful. One of the main reasons for using it was that wine yeasts were far more sensitive to the sugar content of the must than they are today. Indeed, they were so sensitive that they would not ferment satisfactorily – if indeed they would ferment at all – in a must containing more than approximately two pounds of sugar per gallon. For this reason the hydrometer played a far more important role than it does today. However, the role it plays is still important for many people, so it is worthwhile getting to know and understand it, which is quite a simple thing to do. For example, if you start a must fermenting which has a certain specific gravity you can tell once all fermentation has ceased how much alcohol you have made. Further, when doing this, you can always tell when fermentation has ceased altogether and not just 'stuck', as we call it. When we use this expression we mean that fermentation has ceased prematurely, in other words, it has stopped before the desired amount of alcohol has been made. From this you will have guessed that while using the hydrometer, you can adjust the sugar content to give you whatever alcohol content you want with the limit of fifteen per cent. It is agreed that sixteen per cent can be made with suitable musts, yeasts and with constant warmth, but it does not follow automatically that this percentage will be achieved. For this reason it is wise to presume that under ordinary home conditions you will not achieve more than fourteen or fifteen per cent. With my experience, with some skill – or perhaps luck – I have produced wines of eighteen per cent by volume. This involves some painstaking work because it means feeding the fermenting must with small amounts of sugar over rather long periods as the yeast uses up the previous addition.

The first thing to understand when using the hydrometer is the meaning of 'specific gravity'. First of all, when we have prepared a must it has a gravity (density-thickness could be used as a meaning of gravity) and when using the hydrometer we must find what this gravity is as compared with water. We use water as the comparison factor. In other words we use water as the specific. So our musts have a gravity as compared with water – in other words they have a specific gravity. Water has the gravity of 1000. Our musts, because they contain sugar and other matter, will have a higher gravity than water because the sugar makes them thicker, or gives them a higher gravity. Now let us look at the hydrometer. This is merely a weighted float with a scale of readings along the length of it. When this is put into a sample of the must it will sink low or float high depending on the amount of sugar present. The more sugar there is the higher it will float. Conversely, the less sugar there is the lower it will sink. Either way, it will float, and when it floats steadily, you look at the sample at eye level to see where the surface of the must cuts across the stem as shown in the illustration. This figure is the specific gravity of your must.

Having noted the specific gravity and having compared this with the hydrometer table (page 41), you will be able to see how much alcohol this specific gravity will make.

It will be seen in the illustration that the hydrometer is showing a reading of 1080. It will be seen from the table that this reading will give an alcohol content of 10.5 per cent by volume. This is not a high percentage, but it would be enough for the many people who like low alcohol dry wines.

Now let us suppose that you want to increase the specific gravity from 1080 to 1110 to give you a dry wine of 14.5 per cent by volume. The first thing to bear in mind is that $2\frac{1}{4}$ oz. of sugar will raise the reading in one gallon by 5° on the hydrometer, while $4\frac{1}{2}$ oz. will raise it 10°. If, therefore, you want to raise the reading from 1080 to 1110 you must increase the reading by 30° and since $4\frac{1}{2}$ oz. of sugar raises it by 10° it is clear that you will have to add three times $4\frac{1}{2}$ oz. of sugar.

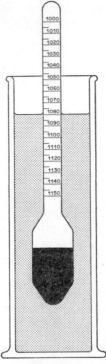

Fig. 11

You will meet up with this sort of reading when using concentrated grape juices, but when taking the reading of musts prepared from ordinary fruits which have been diluted to such an extent that their sugar content has been reduced to practically nil, the specific gravity is likely to be as low as 1020. In such a case you would have to raise the reading to give you whichever alcohol content you want.

When adding sugar to raise the gravity it is always wise to use a little of the strained must for this purpose. If water is used, the overall volume of the must is increased and the result of this would be that you would not obtain the reading you want. So when you have taken the reading and measured out the sugar required, take a little of the juice into a polythene, china or pyrex jug, add the sugar to this and stand the jug in hot water over gentle heat, stirring constantly to dissolve the sugar without heating the fruit juice too much. When all the sugar is dissolved, stir into the must. There is no need to take the reading after you have done this because you will have added the sugar required to give you the specific gravity you want.

When large amounts of sugar are to be added when, for example, the initial specific gravity is low and where, for example, you may have to increase by as much as 90° (40½ oz. sugar) a much larger amount of must will have to be warmed in order to dissolve the sugar.

As I have mentioned, the main aim of most amateurs in using the hydrometer is to make sure that they have made as much alcohol as they set out to.

Hydrometer Table

Specific Gravity	Alcohol by volume per cent	Per cent proof
1040	5.0	8.8
1050	6.4	10.5
1060	7.7	12.6
1070	9.0	15.7
1080	10.5	17.6
1090	11.9	21.4
1100	13.4	22.5
1110	14.5	24.9
1120	16.0	28.0

(This table does not cover the complete range but it is the range within which you will be working.)

Now let us look at the hydrometer table. You will see that this ends at the specific gravity of 1120 with the corresponding alcohol content of 16.0. And there is no reason why with care this amount of alcohol should not be made. But this is too high for dry wine – though some people like them like this – so it is best if you propose to make this amount of alcohol to add a further 4½ oz. of sugar per gallon to sweeten the wine.

This will in effect (whether you take the reading or not) give you a specific gravity of 1130. What we must now bear in mind is this: the yeast will use up sugar in the ordinary way during a good fermentation to the extent of 1110° on the hydrometer; under very good conditions it will use up 1120°. So, in the first instance you will when starting with a gravity of 1110 end up with a dry wine of 14.5 per cent of alcohol by volume. In the second you may end up with 14.5 per cent alcohol with 10° (4½ oz. sugar) left unfermented. If, as I have suggested above, you aim at 16 per cent by volume by starting with a gravity of 1120 and then adding 4½ oz. sugar to give you a reading of 1130, with the idea of having 4½ oz. of sugar left unfermented to sweeten the wine, and the yeast did not perform with the required vigour, you might have more than 4½ oz. of unfermented sugar to sweeten because the yeast may have made only 15 per cent of alcohol.

This was my reason earlier in these pages for advising you not to expect more than 14 per cent to 15 per cent of alcohol by volume.

The following table will clarify what I mean:

Sugar Table

Starting Gravity	Gravity at the end of fermentation	Type of wine
1080	1000	dry
1090	1000	dry
1100	1000	dry
1110	possibly 1000	dry if fermentation good
1120	1000—possibly 1005	reasonably dry
1130	1010—possibly 1015	medium sweet
1140	1020—possibly 1025	definitely sweet

From this you can see that while you can adjust the sugar in a must to give you the amount of alcohol you want, care should be taken to allow for the fact that the yeast might not make quite so much alcohol as you hoped for.

An important fact to bear in mind when using the hydrometer is that the must is not made up merely of sugar and
water. Also present are pectins whether active or not, acids,
tannin and other matter, and all these register on the hydrometer as if they were sugar. Some allowance will have to be
made for this if absolute accuracy is important to you. A
further point is what is known as surface tension. This is
shown here.

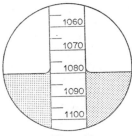

Fig. 12

Obviously because of the surface tension and the matter in
the must which registers on the hydrometer as sugar, it is
wise to allow 5° on the hydrometer for this and regard all
initial readings to be 5° less than they actually are. Using
the hydrometer with concentrated grape juices is covered in
the section on using concentrated grape juices (page 56).

Seven

Processes after Fermentation

Preserving and Fortifying

Preserving wine is a simple and inexpensive means of preventing re-fermentation where this could happen in a finished wine such as when it has been sweetened or when a low alcohol sweet wine has been produced. A bone-dry wine will not ferment again once it has ceased because there is no fermented sugar present for a stray yeast cell to work upon. But it could, like the sweet ones mentioned above, be unstable. These are similar to what are known as unstable explosives – they are likely to go off at any time. Where the maximum alcohol is made such as when a good yeast is used and constant warmth is given with the use of a heated fermentation cupboard, all the wines should be stable.

Many people preserve their wines as a matter of course and while this is sensible it should not be necessary where, as I have mentioned, the maximum alcohol has been made. However, and because not all of you will be sure that you have indeed made the maximum alcohol it would be sensible to preserve your wines just to be on the safe side, and this should be done immediately after you are satisfied that fermentation has ceased. I recommend this because the Campden tablet will produce a slight haze in the wine, and this haze will settle out with the others that will doubtless be present at this stage of production. All that has to be done is to take one Campden tablet per gallon of wine to be treated. Crush this to a fine powder, take a small sample of the wine and dissolve the powder thoroughly in this and then stir this sample into the bulk. If you are racking at this stage it would be a good idea to put the treated sample into the empty jar and siphon the wine into this and so be assured of thorough mixing of the preservative. Wines treated in this fashion must still be bunged down tightly during storage and the bottles sealed at bottling time.

Preserving will not flavour the wine because very little is being used, only approximately one-eighth of the amount allowed by law in alcohol wines. Many people use two tablets per gallon to be doubly sure of preserving without there being any hint of the flavour of the preservative in the finished wine.

Fortifying wines with spirit can prove expensive. But it has the advantage that it not only preserves, but that it also increases the alcohol content by one or two per cent, and many people feel that the expense is well worthwhile where they have turned out a quite exceptional vintage. They reason that a couple of ounces of spirit in a few bottles to be put away for a long time for some special occasion is a sensible thing to do because it improves the wine so greatly over the years.

Only a spirit with neither colour nor flavour should be used for this purpose for the very simple reason that it will not alter the colour or flavour of the wine. Whisky or brandy or for that matter any other flavoured spirit would spoil the natural flavour of the wine and no matter how strenuously you might deny it your friends will know what you have done.

Vodka being both colourless and flavourless is ideal for our purpose. Other spirits in the same category are much higher in alcohol – Polish Pure spirit being twice as strong. But there is no saving in using them because you pay for the alcohol content, the higher it is the more you pay.

A full-size bottle of vodka contains 26⅔ fl. oz. From this and by studying the following table you will be able to see how much fortifying will cost. This table is for use with the standard British wine bottle which holds the same as the full-size bottle of vodka. If you use the shoulderless continental type bottle which holds 22 fl. oz. the table will not apply to them strictly and because these hold less than the British standard bottle you would, if you used the same amount of spirit, raise the alcohol content a little more.

Because I do not know in advance how much alcohol your

wines contain, I am presuming that they contain the average
alcohol for home-made wines and have compiled the table
accordingly. You will see that I have put this figure at 14 per
cent by volume, and that I refer to the vodka as being 40 per
cent by volume (70° proof being 40 per cent by volume).

Add fl. oz. vodka	to these fl. oz. of wines	to give one 26 oz. bottle of per cent by vol.	Degrees proof
1	25	15	26.2
2	24	16	28.0
3	23	17	29.7
4	22	18	31.4
5	21	19	33.1
6	20	20	35.0

This is as far as the table need go. I say this because there
really is no point in fortifying above seventeen or eighteen
per cent because this is plenty for any kind of wine. Ports,
good sherries and Vermouth are around eighteen per cent
by volume and as most of you will know from sampling them
this is a high percentage. Indeed, when I fortify – which I
often do – I do not increase to above sixteen per cent.

A further point to consider when fortifying is that if you
add a lot of spirit you will reduce the flavour of the wine.
This might not matter with a fully-flavoured robust wine, but
it would with a mildly-flavoured one. If you must increase to
above eighteen per cent it would be best to use Polish Pure
spirit, which, as I have mentioned, is twice as strong, and use
half the amounts of spirit shown in the table.

Storing and maturing

Storage space is very often a problem not only for beginners
but also for those who make quite large amounts regularly.
For most people the cupboard under the stairs is the best
place and this is quite suitable. Bear in mind that any storage
area high up is always warmer than an area near the floor or

on the floor itself. Obviously, high shelving in a warm room, or a cool room for that matter, would be detrimental to wines.

The storage area should be cool, dark and damp-free. Many serious wine-makers build themselves 'cellars' in a variety of unlikely places – one man wrote to me, saying that he had over seven hundred bottles in a concrete-floored brick-built shed sandwiched between two outbuildings which keep his 'cellar' cool.

But the storage area for most people need not be as elaborate as this. The fact remains, however, that the longer you are making wines the more storage space you will need, and it can be almost anywhere so long as it is cool, dark and dry. Coal bunkers no longer used for coal, cool corners of sheds or outhouses shaded from the sun are other spaces that come to mind. Doubtless many people will find their own storage space quite easily An insulated loft is one idea that was put to me some years ago and this, of course, is ideal. Much will depend on the number of jars to be stored and their size and you would be surprised how little space they need. Bottled wines either in special bins or in cardboard crates stored in the spare room is very often the bottled-wine store. Wine-makers are immensely resourceful and it would be a poor wine-maker indeed who could not find space for the wine he has made.

A period of storage in bulk is always beneficial to wines of any sort for it is during this period that many changes take place. Indeed, wine-making is such a continuous process that not until the wine has had time to mature in bulk and then finish maturing in bottles can it be regarded as a finished product. *When* a wine has matured is probably the hardest thing for anybody to decide except perhaps the most experienced wine-maker. It is, I am sure, merely a matter of judgement based upon previous experience. But since each wine will be different in all respects from the time the must is prepared until the wine is finally decanted for use, each wine will have to be judged on its merits. One year your elderberry wine or blackberry wine will be absolutely delightful after a few months. But it will improve greatly if kept a long time – say three to four years. But this does not mean that if you like it six months old, you cannot use it – of course you can. The same applies to all other wines. However, elderberry and some others are usually a bit rough to the palate at an early stage so it is best to leave those you know will be like this until they have had time to mellow down. This roughness is most often caused by an excess of tannin which will frequently colour glass storage jars from pink to dark red or brown. This excess takes a long time to settle out, but because it is confined mainly to elderberries and a few other English dark-skinned fruits from hedgerow and garden it is not too frequently encountered.

Generally speaking, those in their early days of wine-making may use their wines after six months. They will know instinctively upon tasting that the wine will improve if kept longer. The wise wine-maker will make sufficient to enable him to use some of it after six months or so while some is put away for a year or two. He can continue this process by bottling the two- or three-year-old wine as the new wine is put into store. And he will, eventually, be able to leave a few gallons for five or even ten years – and he will be glad he did so.

During the period of storage in bulk, chemical reactions are constantly taking place, flavours are changing slightly and improved upon. Esters are formed and bouquet develops and during the period or part of it, it is important that oxygen reaches the wine to help these changes take place. When stored in barrels oxygen percolates through the pores of the wood, but when in jars only the bung will facilitate this function. But it is enough. Small quantities of wine mature more quickly than larger amounts. So it is quite in order to cut off the oxygen supply to small lots of say one to two gallons after six to nine months if you propose to keep them longer. This is done by slicing the bung off level with the top of the jar and covering the whole area with sealing wax. If this is not done, there is the chance of over-oxidation (an excess of oxygen reaching the wine) so that there is risk of the wine becoming flat and lifeless.

As mentioned, wines should be kept in the dark while maturing. When bottling, red wines should be put into dark glass bottles, either brown or green, along with the paler coloured red and pink varieties such as rosé. It has always been accepted that the paler reds and rosé types would not be harmed in clear glass bottles but I have discovered that they can be if light reaches them for too long. The dark to medium reds are affected adversely by light if it reaches them for months upon end, so do use dark bottles for all red wines. The pale golden sorts, and white wines, may be stored in clear glass bottles. Naturally, all wines benefit if they are kept in darker than ordinary daylight. Direct sunlight for short periods can spoil a great many wines. Perhaps this is the reason some of the 'plonk' bought from supermarkets is so rubbishy.

Blending

Blending is often a sensible means of ironing out faults in finished wines. And it is very often the only means of obtaining some special results for which you might be aiming. In the latter case, blending finished wines very often gives you the clues necessary for evolving recipes for making some really out of the ordinary wines. Do not imagine that just because there are thousands of recipes available today that there will not be a lot of new ones tomorrow. This is how new recipes come about. One reader makes a decent wine which he shares with a friend. That friend has a wine which he thinks will blend well with the wine belonging to his friend and so they talk it over between themselves, discussing the various ingredients they used and how they made the wines. They then consider what is likely to be the result if they use a certain group of ingredients – say three or four different sorts and they set to work. They will of course take into account the fact that one or perhaps two of the ingredients will produce acid, while another will produce tannin, another will give the required basic flavour and the fourth produce a pleasant background flavour and effect the required aroma and bouquet. And then they will decide to add such as bananas to give extra body without putting too much flavour into the wine. Raisins will give body, but to obtain this in sufficient quantity when using raisins at least one pound per gallon has to be used with the result that the flavour of raisins is noticeable in the finished wine. If this flavour is required, then of course it does not matter, but it is not a flavour that goes down well or blends well with other flavours in certain wines. Sultanas are a different matter, they will add body without adding much noticeable flavour to a wine unless they are used in rather large amounts.

This sort of blending for the purpose of evolving new recipes is best left until you are experienced enough to be able to judge with reasonable certainty precisely how each ingredient will play its part in the build-up of the complex system of flavours, aromas and bouquets that form a finished wine. And this can only be done by careful sampling. By sampling I mean tasting with the will to find out exactly what there is in wine besides the flavour that pleases the palate and the slight warming sensation produced by the alcohol present. And the only way you can do this is to sip slowly, chew the wine, roll it round the mouth preferably with the eyes closed. You will be surprised when you do this with a variety of wines how vastly each differs from the next. It is sensible to do this with every wine you make, taking several samples and tasting them as just described. When you do this, clear the palate between samples with either a piece of cheese or plain dry biscuit chewed thoroughly. And never put a sample of wine on to the dregs of the previous sample. Always use a new glass for each new wine.

Blending for the purpose of ironing out faults in finished wines is common practice – and a very sensible one at that. Many wines that are disappointing for one reason or another can be blended carefully with one or perhaps two others that will make the disappointing one quite a good wine without spoiling the others. Take for example a common fault caused mainly by using under-ripe fruits. The wine is over-acid. True, this can be rectified by using precipitated chalk, but treatment of finished wines in this fashion is best avoided if possible. Therefore, blending a slightly acid wine with a similar wine which lacks acid to a slight degree will improve both. Similarly, an over-sweet wine – which is a fault not easily remedied in any other way – will be improved vastly by careful blending with a dry wine. But the wines to be blended must always be similar otherwise there will be a conflict of flavours.

As a guide to this, most hedgerow and garden fruits which produce red wines will blend well together. Similar fruits which produce white wines will also blend well together. Root wines will blend well together, and with wines made from citrus fruits such as oranges and lemons. Flower wines with their aromatic and delicate flavours are not such an easy matter to blend. Wines made from dried fruits blend well together and often with root wines and some ordinary fruit wines made from hedgerow and garden fruits. It really is a matter of common sense. Any reader who has sampled his wines in the manner described in this section should be able to tell almost at once which wines will blend well and those that will not. Blending is not just a matter of sploshing a couple of bottles of wine together. It need not be a pains-taking operation, but if you want good results – and you would not be contemplating blending if you do not – it pays to approach the job sensibly.

The first thing to do is to get hold of two fluid-ounce measures – they are quite cheap. Then decide which wine needs more of the second wine to improve it. For example, if a wine is much over-acid you will need more of the wine which lacks acid to strike a balance. The same applies with an over-sweet wine, this will require more of the dry sort. Or, if you plan to blend a too dry wine with a too sweet one, you must find out by sampling how much of each is needed to give the result you are looking for. This is where the two fluid-ounce measures come in. These are marked with both tea-spoons and millilitres as well so that you can work according to personal whim. Either way, first measure an equal quantity of each wine into both measures and then pour them into a small glass of the Paris Goblet type. The glass must be clean and brightly polished. Sample the blend after swirling the contents around the glass. And don't forget to roll it round the mouth and chew it before swallowing slowly.

From this sample you will be able to tell which of more wine is required and roughly how much. Wash and dry the measures and the glass and start again using a little more of the wine you have decided is the one most needed. And do not forget to chew a little cheese between samples otherwise the slight differences in the blends may not be noticeable.

The whole idea when doing this sort of thing is to use as little wine as possible, say, half a fluid ounce of each to start with. It is wise too, to have someone on hand to help with the sampling. I have never found any difficulty in persuading a couple of friends to come round for a sampling party. If you mention tactfully that they might bring a couple of bottles to try blending at the same time, quite a jolly evening often results. In fact, what started out as a serious evening's work often turned out to be quite hilarious with wives joining in as well. But we enjoyed it and found the right blends at the same time. And so can you.

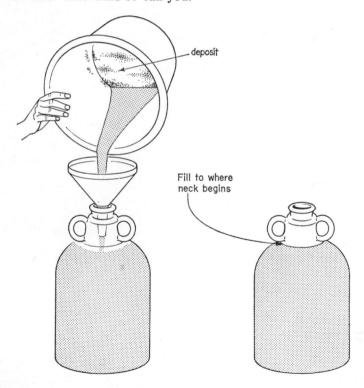

Fig. 12(a) and (b)

Eight

Making Wines in a Flat or Quickly-made Wines

Making wines in a flat or other limited accommodation may not seem to be a feasible proposition, but it is, and a very rewarding one at that. People living in this sort of accommodation cannot for obvious reasons have their wines in store for many months – indeed, they need to be able to make good wines and use them up in rather a short time so that not only do they have some ready for use quickly, but also have some fermenting to replace what has been used up. A constant cycle can easily be maintained to achieve this end and it does not necessarily mean drinking inferior or immature products. It simply means using suitable ingredients with the latest utensils designed to speed fermentation so that a two- or three-gallon batch is ready for use eight or nine weeks from starting out. Once the cycle has been started it means that after eight or nine weeks you can have a constant supply of very good-quality wines always on hand.

A three-gallon batch will give you eighteen standard British wine bottles. Where continental bottles of the shoulderless type are used, you will obtain from twenty-one to twenty-four bottles. And if you are fond of dry wines you might have this amount ready for use in as little as six weeks from starting out. This is because less sugar is used and therefore fermentation is over in less time than where the maximum alcohol is required for such as sweet wines.

As I have mentioned, dry wines are better for being in the range of eleven or twelve per cent alcohol by volume, and if a fermentation cupboard is used (see page 29) this amount should be made quite quickly. But you will make it even more quickly if you use a three-gallon fermentation vessel fitted with a thermostatically controlled heater (see Fig. 13). Where central heating is installed this sort of thing would not be necessary during winter, but it would be most helpful during summer when the central heating is not in use and the cool of night time would have the effect of prolonging fermentation.

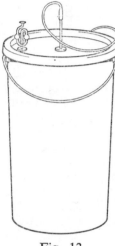

Fig. 13

Do bear in mind that I am not encouraging you to use expensive equipment just for the sake of it. I am suggesting its use – if indeed it can be considered expensive in the light of its value – for the sake of enabling you to make your wines quickly.

Obviously, people living in flats for whom this chapter is designed will most likely be living in the larger towns and cities where ingredients from the hedgerows and fields are not within their reach. Therefore we must look to ingredients which are readily available from the corner shop or from the many home wine-making supply stores that have sprung up in recent years – there being at least one in most towns and many in the larger cities. Health food stores and major multiple chemists are now stockists of concentrated grape juices and most of the main items required in wine-making. Supermarkets, quite unwittingly, perhaps, are also a source of supply of quick wine-making ingredients; orange or grapefruit juices, canned prunes and suchlike. But let me deal with concentrated grape juices first.

The most important consideration when using concentrated grape juices is that they contain a lot of sugar. Each range offered by the various supply firms is almost identical in that the types are called Burgundy-style, Rosé, Hock, Muscat and so on. I have tried most of them and I must confess that I obtain much better wines from some than I do from others. But all make the type of wine that the supplier claims they do. Most offer a sherry type, but I have not been successful in making a genuine sherry – though I have on occasion produced an imitation.

It will be found that most of the concentrated grape juices available, when diluted with water to one gallon, have a specific gravity of 1065. Now, if you will look at the hydrometer table on page 41 you will see that this specific gravity will give you an alcohol content of between 7.7 per cent and 9.0 per cent by volume or between 12.6° and 15.7° proof. Actually the figure 1065, which is not on the hydrometer table, will give you 8.4 per cent by volume or 14.0° proof. Obviously, this is not enough even for a dry wine which is always better for being rather lower than average in alcohol content. On the whole, I feel that to raise the reading to 1100 for a dry wine would be the most sensible practice, though of course you can raise to a mere 1090 if you wish and make the corresponding alcohol content as required. This of course applies to dry wines. Where sweet or medium sweet wines are your pleasure it is best to raise the gravity to 1110 and to add a little sugar, say about four ounces for sweetening purposes. As will be seen, 1110 specific gravity will give you 14.5 per cent by volume. If you are using all the modern aids to fermentation then you could safely raise the gravity to 1120 and then add further sugar for sweetening purposes. The decision must rest with you because you know what sort of wine you want and in the light of the sort of utensils you are using whether

you will make 15 per cent or 16 per cent by volume. If
you will take a look at the sugar table on page 42 you will
see what I mean.

What puzzles me about most of the methods printed on the
reverse side of the labels on the cans of concentrated grape
juice is that they are mostly troublesome and clumsy. I
have tried them, naturally, but I tired of them and evolved
a simple, trouble-free method which is not only quicker but
produces better wines. I have had my method tested by a few
knowledgeable friends who agree that they prefer my method.[1]

You will find that one particular range of concentrates is
so prepared that it will give a certain percentage of alcohol and
that unfermentable substances added will give sweetness to
the finished wine. So my method would not necessarily apply
to this range.

Using Concentrated Grape Juices[1]

It will be seen that most concentrates come in 1 kg. size cans
(2lb. 3oz.). Some weigh just a little more. The Hidalgo range
is a much heavier concentrate and I will deal with this range
separately.

The procedure without using the hydrometer is as follows;
but do bear in mind that you will have to consult the hydrometer table to find how much you want to raise the gravity
from the figure of 1065 which is the most likely specific
gravity of the juice in its diluted form as one gallon of must –
the amount we shall have when all initial operations are
complete. I usually boil one gallon of water about eight hours
before I open the can of concentrate to ensure that the water
is cool when I shall need it. I then calculate how much I want
to raise the gravity (from 1065 to whatever reading I want) and
measure out the sugar. This I put into about a quart of water
in a saucepan and bring it slowly to the boil stirring constantly
to ensure that it does not settle to the bottom and burn or
solidify. When this is boiling, I cut off the heat and leave it
covered until I need it. Hours later when I know the water

[1] Please note this method © H. E. Bravery, 1973.

is cool and the syrup cooled well, I sterilise my fermenting vessel, wipe the can of concentrate with a damp cloth, open it and pour into the fermenting vessel. Some sugary concentrate occasionally sticks to the can and this can be softened by some of the boiled water. Do make sure you remove all the concentrate from the can. Having done this, stir in the sugar syrup and then make up to one gallon. Obviously a fermentation vessel marked in half gallons and gallons will be helpful here. Having done this, I give the must a thorough stirring, add half a Campden tablet which has been crushed and dissolved in a little warm water, and then give the must a further stirring. I then add my prepared yeast starter. The vessel is then covered as already advised and put into the fermentation cupboard. After seven or eight days, the still fermenting wine is poured very carefully into a gallon jar while leaving as much of the deposit in the fermenting vessel as possible. The jar is then filled to where the neck begins with a little boiled cooled water, a fermentation lock is then fitted and the wine not interfered with again until all fermentation has ceased.

If you decide to use the hydrometer the method is practically the same except that you will not prepare any sugar beforehand. But the water should be boiled and allowed to cool. The can of concentrate is then poured into the fermenting vessel and made up to one gallon with the boiled cooled water. The hydrometer flask is then filled halfway with some of the must and the hydrometer lowered into it. More sample is added until the hydrometer floats clear of all parts of the flask while it is standing on a level surface. The reading is then taken as described in the chapter on using the hydrometer. The amount of sugar to use is then calculated and measured out. This is put into a saucepan with about a quart of the diluted concentrate and heated very gently, stirring constantly to dissolve the sugar and at the same time avoid over-heating the juice which might spoil the natural flavour. When the sugar is dissolved the syrup is stirred into the must.

The next operation is to give the must a thorough stirring, add half a Campden tablet as advised in the previous method, give another stirring and then add the yeast, cover as already advised. And then proceed as for the method above.

These two methods have been evolved for their simplicity and easy application by anybody. I work much more precisely at times and with certain concentrates, but to put all the details down here would only complicate matters and confuse you. If you follow either of these methods I am sure you will be delighted with the results.

The Hidalgo range of concentrates does not follow the pattern of Hocks, Rosés, Burgundies and so on. Their range is unique. And as mentioned the concentrate is heavier, having a specific gravity in its concentrated form of 1400. When a quart can of this is made up to one gallon with water it will have a specific gravity of 1100. Therefore, if a dry wine of 13.4 per cent of alcohol by volume is required, no sugar at all need be added.

The quickly-made wines aspect of this chapter comes mainly from making dry wines with concentrated grape juices, canned fruit and canned fruit juices from supermarkets or other sources. Notable examples of these are canned peaches and canned apricots, prunes, and canned orange or grapefruit juices. Using this sort of material means opening a can and starting off at once.

The whole idea of making these wines dry is to have fermentation over quickly. You may then use them as they are or sweeten them to taste. How to do this is explained after the recipes and methods here. However, if you do intend to sweeten these after having made them as dry wines, do use an extra seven or eight ounce can of whichever fruit you are using (and do this at the beginning) otherwise the wine may lack the fuller flavour required of a sweeter wine.

Apricot or Peach Wine (Dry, light and fresh in flavour)

Two 15 oz. cans of either apricots or peaches (in syrup), $1\frac{3}{4}$ lb. sugar, $\frac{1}{2}$ level teaspoonful Pectinol, yeast of your choice, and water as in method.

Put the sugar in about a pint of water in a saucepan and bring it slowly to the boil stirring frequently to ensure that the sugar does not settle and stick to the saucepan. Boil also about six pints of water and let both this and the sugar syrup cool well (about 3 hours). When cooled, pour the canned fruits into the fermenting vessel and crush them by hand. Then add the syrup and water and mix well together. Crush one Campden fruit preserving tablet to a powder and dissolve in about an eggcupful of warm water and stir this into the pulp. Give the mixture a thorough stirring – thirty seconds is not too long – and then add the yeast and nutrient. Cover as advised and put the mixture in the warm. Within twelve hours fermentation will be under way; it could be a lot less than twelve hours depending on the sort of yeast you are using. Leave in the warm to ferment for seven days stirring daily.

The next step is to strain out the pulp through two or three thicknesses of muslin and to press this as dry as you can, then clean the fermenting vessel and return the strained wine to this. At the same time add the Pectinol. Having done this return the wine, covered as before, to its warm place for three or four more days. Then pour very carefully into a gallon jar leaving as much deposit in the pail as you can. If the jar is not filled to where the neck begins, fill to this level with boiled cooled water, then fit a fermentation lock and leave in the warm until all fermentation has ceased.

Pineapple Wine

This is rather an acid wine, as acid as some wines from the continent, so it is not everybody's cup of tea. However, if you feel you would like this, bearing in mind the flavour of pineapple, use the method for peach or apricot wine and use two 15 oz. cans of pineapple, but do chop the rings or chunks well before adding the sugar and water.

Prune Wine

Three 15 oz. cans of prunes, the strained juice of 2 lemons, $1\frac{1}{2}$ lb. sugar, $\frac{1}{2}$ level teaspoonful Pectinol, yeast of your choice, nutrient and water as in method.

Use the method for apricot or peach wine, but add the strained lemon juice at the same time as the sugar and water. Use about one pint less water to begin with.

Orange Wine

Two 15 oz. cans of orange juice, 2 lb. sugar, $\frac{1}{2}$ level teaspoonful of Pectinol, yeast of your choice, nutrient and water as in method.

Put the sugar in a saucepan with about a quart of water and bring slowly to the boil stirring frequently to prevent the sugar settling and sticking to the saucepan. At the same time boil about four pints of water and leave this and the syrup to cool. When cool, pour the orange juice into the fermenting vessel, add the syrup and water, give a thorough stirring and add the yeast and nutrient. *Do not* use a Campden tablet. Cover the vessel as advised and put the mixture in a warm place to ferment for seven days, stirring daily. Stir in the Pectinol on the last day. Having done this, pour very carefully into a gallon jar leaving as much deposit in the fermenting vessel as you can. If the jar is not filled to where the neck begins, fill to this level with boiled cooled water, then fit a fermentation lock and leave in the warm until all fermentation has ceased.

Loganberry or Blackberry Wine (Light, fresh and fruity)

Two 15 oz. cans of either loganberries or blackberries, $1\frac{3}{4}$ lb. sugar, strained juice of one lemon, $\frac{1}{2}$ level teaspoonful Pectinol, yeast of your choice, nutrient, and water as in method.

Put the sugar in the fermenting vessel. Pour the fruits into a saucepan with a little water and bring just to boiling and simmer for a few minutes. Pour over the sugar and stir until sugar is dissolved. Then make the mixture up to roughly a gallon with boiling water. Cover and allow the mixture to cool well, then add the yeast and nutrient, and Pectinol. Cover as advised and put the wine in the warm to ferment for seven days. After this, strain through muslin or similar material and allow the wine to stand covered for about an hour. Then pour carefully into a gallon jar leaving as much deposit behind as you can. If the jar is not filled to where the neck begins, fill to this level with boiled cooled water. Then fit a fermentation lock and leave until all fermentation has ceased.

Sweetening Quickly-Made Wines

If you decide to sweeten these wines do be sure that they are brilliantly clear before doing so. You will need one to two teaspoonfuls of sugar to each bottle, bearing in mind that there are six standard wine bottles to the gallon. Take about a pint of the wine, pour this into a china or polythene jug, add the sugar and stir well in. Stand the jug in a saucepan of water over gentle heat and heat slowly, stirring the wine all the time so that the sugar dissolves without the wine becoming too warm. When the sugar is dissolved, mix the treated wine with the rest. It is best if you can put the treated wine in an empty jar and fill up with the remainder of the wine. This ensures good distribution of the sugar. Sample the wine and if it is not quite sweet enough, repeat the process being careful not to over-sweeten.

Having sweetened a wine in this fashion there is always the risk that the added sugar might give rise to renewed fermentation, so it is wise to preserve these wines as described in the section on preserving wines (page 44).

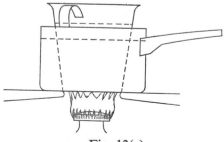

Fig. 13(a)

Nine

Making Fruit Wines by the Heat Treatment Method

This method lost a good deal of popularity when the sulphiting method was discovered and the reason is easy to understand. Years ago heating the fruits to sterilise them gave rise to pectin in the must and therefore the finished wine. This holds minute solids in suspension to form a permanent cloudiness. The old remedy for this was to strain out every particle of pectin-bearing fruit through a jelly bag before heating it. This is a tedious job no longer necessary because we use a pectin-destroying enzyme during the process and this ensures that the pectin cannot cloud our wines. Pectinol is now part of most fruit wine recipes to be used with the heat treatment method because it is this that destroys pectin, assuring us of a brilliantly clear wine. Do not add the Pectinol earlier than stated in the methods. Because of the availability of pectin-destroying enzymes this method has become popular again. The popularity of this method is easy to understand because the flavour of wines made from what we might call stewed fruit really is enchanting. Not all fruits are suitable for this method, but most garden and hedgerow fruits certainly are. Lovers of wines flavoured by raw fruits should use the recipes and methods in chapter 10.

It will be seen that I give two recipes for each fruit – one for dry wine and another for sweet, and provided fermentation is as satisfactory as it should be, the dry will be bone dry and the sweet sweet without being over-sweet. The recipes are followed immediately by one method which is suitable for both recipes for that particular fruit. Doing it this way allows me much more space to give you a wider range of recipes and methods throughout the book and cover a far wider range of ingredients than would be possible if I had to write out a fully detailed method with each recipe. So all you have to do is to select the recipe which you feel will make the type of wine you will like, either dry or sweet, and then follow the method, which comes immediately after the recipe.

Using Concentrated Grape Juices with the Recipes in this Chapter

It will be seen that I include a small amount of concentrated grape juice in the recipes in this chapter. But it does *not* mean that you have to use it. The recipes will make excellent wines without this additive, but the wines will be just that much better if you use the grape juice recommended. There seems to be some criticism today of what are termed as 'one-fruit recipes', suggesting that recipes calling for one fruit only cannot make wines of quality. I find this hard to understand when I have had literally hundreds of letters from readers of my other books who have won prizes at wine shows with my one-fruit recipes. I myself won first prize with a one-fruit recipe (blackberry) at the first National Conference and Show of Amateur Wine-makers at Bournemouth in 1960 (a six-hundred bottle show). However, it does seem that over the years, and with the availability of new types of ingredients and as the result of experimentation, mixtures of ingredients do sometimes make better wines. Those of you who are completely new to wine-making are advised to omit the grape juice in these recipes in order to find out for yourself just what excellent wines are made from the basic ingredients. Later, when you have a little more experience, you may use grape juices, raisins, sultanas or bananas as additives or you may use the special recipes in chapter 11 which are designed for the more experienced wine-maker.

It will be seen in the recipes that the grape juice is set in brackets. A second amount of sugar is also set in brackets. If

you do not use the grape juice, do not use the second amount
of sugar. In other words, leave out the two items in brackets
and follow the basic recipe. The second amount of sugar is
there because if you use grape juice the sugar it contains must
be accounted for. *Note*: The sugar in concentrated grape
juices tends to settle at the bottom of the can. To dissolve this
so that it is dispersed before use, open the can and stand it
in hot water, stirring until the sugar is well dissolved. Then
measure out the amount to be used and put the rest in a
small Kilner jar, screw on the cap tightly and use this as soon
as possible for another batch of wine.

Loganberry Wines

Dry. 3 lb. loganberries, ($\frac{1}{2}$ pt. Rosé concentrate), $2\frac{1}{4}$ lb. sugar,
($1\frac{3}{4}$ lb. sugar), all-purpose wine yeast, nutrient, $\frac{1}{2}$ level teaspoonful Pectinol, water as in method.

Sweet. 4 lb. loganberries, ($\frac{1}{2}$ pt. Rosé concentrate), 3 lb. sugar,
($2\frac{1}{2}$ lb. sugar), all-purpose wine yeast, nutrient, $\frac{1}{2}$ level teaspoonful Pectinol, water as in method.

Hull the fruits, rinse them under a fast running tap, then
put them in a saucepan with water to cover them, bring slowly
to the boil stirring occasionally and then simmer gently until
pulpy. Put the sugar in the fermenting pail and pour on the
hot fruit, stir until the sugar is dissolved. Then make up to
about nine pints with boiling water. Cover well, and leave
the mixture to cool to lukewarm.

Having done this, crush half a Campden fruit preserving
tablet to a powder, dissolve this in about a cupful of the
juice and mix it thoroughly into the bulk.

Add the grape juice if being used and in any case give the
mixture a thorough stirring. Finally, add the yeast, nutrient
and Pectinol and stir in. Cover as advised and leave in the
warm to ferment for seven or eight days, stirring daily. After
this, strain the pulp through three or four thicknesses of
muslin and wring out tightly. Clean the fermenting vessel
and return the wine to this, cover as before and leave for a
further three or four days. Then pour carefully into a gallon
jar (warmed) leaving as much deposit in the pail as you can.

Then fill the jar to where the neck begins, if necessary, with boiled cooled water, fit a fermentation lock and leave until all fermentation has ceased.

Blackcurrant Wines

Dry. 3 lb. blackcurrants, (1 pt. Burgundy concentrate), $2\frac{1}{4}$ lb. sugar, ($1\frac{1}{4}$ lb. sugar), all-purpose wine yeast, nutrient, $\frac{1}{2}$ level teaspoonful Pectinol, water as in method.

Sweet. $3\frac{1}{2}$ lb. blackcurrants, (1 pt. Burgundy concentrate), 3 lb. sugar, (2 lb. sugar), all-purpose wine yeast, nutrient, $\frac{1}{2}$ level teaspoonful Pectinol, water as in method.

Remove stalks and rinse the fruits under a fast running tap. Put them in a saucepan with enough water to cover and bring them slowly to the boil, then simmer gently until tender and broken. Put the sugar in the fermenting pail and pour on the near boiling currants. Stir the mixture until the sugar is dissolved and then make up to about nine pints with boiling water. Cover well and leave the mixture to cool to lukewarm. The next step is to crush and dissolve half a Campden fruit preserving tablet in about a cupful of the juice and then mix this with the rest. Stir in the concentrate if being used and give the mixture a thorough stirring.

The next step is to stir in the Pectinol, yeast, and nutrient. Having done this, cover as advised and leave in the warm to ferment for seven or eight days stirring daily. Then strain through three or four thicknesses of muslin and wring out all the juice. Clean the fermenting vessel and return the strained wine to this. Cover as before and leave in the warm for a further two to three days. Then pour carefully into a warmed gallon jar leaving as much deposit in the pail as you can. If the jar is not filled to where the neck begins, fill to this level with boiled cooled water, then fit a fermentation lock and leave until all fermentation has ceased.

Blackberry Wines

Dry. 4 lb. blackberries, ($\frac{3}{4}$ pt. Burgundy concentrate), $2\frac{1}{4}$ lb.

sugar, (1½ lb. sugar), all-purpose wine yeast, nutrient, ½ level teaspoonful Pectinol, water as in method.

Sweet. 4 to 5 lb. blackberries, (1 pt. Burgundy concentrate), 3 lb. sugar, (2 lb. sugar), all-purpose wine yeast, nutrient, ½ level teaspoonful Pectinol, water as in method.

Hull the fruits and rinse them under a fast running tap. Put them in a saucepan with enough water to cover them, bring slowly to the boil and simmer gently until nearly cooked. Put the sugar in the fermenting vessel and pour over the boiling berries, stirring until the sugar is dissolved. Then make up to about nine pints with boiling water. Cover well and leave the mixture to cool to lukewarm. Crush half a Campden fruit preserving tablet to a powder, dissolve this in about a cupful of the juice and then mix it well with the bulk. Stir in the concentrate if being used and give the mixture a thorough stirring. Having done this stir in the Pectinol, yeast and nutrient. Cover as advised and leave in the warm to ferment for seven or eight days, stirring daily. Then strain through three of four thicknesses of muslin and wring out as dry as you can. Clean the fermenting vessel and return the strained wine to this. Cover as before and leave in the warm for a further three or four days. Having done this, pour carefully into a warmed gallon jar leaving as much deposit in the pail as you can. If the jar is not full to where the neck begins, fill to this level with boiled cooled water, then fit a fermentation lock and leave until all fermentation has ceased.

Gooseberry Wines

Dry. 3 lb. gooseberries, (¾ pt. Hock concentrate), 2¼ lb. sugar, (1½ lb. sugar), all-purpose wine yeast, nutrient, ½ level teaspoonful Pectinol, water as in method.

Sweet. 3½ to 4 lb. gooseberries, (¾ pt. Hock concentrate), 3 lb. sugar, (2¼ lb. sugar), all-purpose wine yeast, nutrient, ½ level teaspoonful Pectinol, water as in method.

Top and tail the gooseberries, and rinse them under a fast running tap. Put them in a saucepan with enough water to cover them, bring to the boil and simmer until soft and broken. Put the sugar in the fermenting vessel and pour over the boiling berries, stirring until the sugar is dissolved. Then make up nine pints with boiling water. Cover well and leave the mixture to cool to lukewarm. Then crush one Campden tablet to a powder and dissolve this in about a cupful of the juice and mix this with the bulk. Stir in the concentrate if being used and give the whole a thorough stirring. The next step is to stir in the nutrient, yeast and Pectinol. Cover the vessel as advised and leave in the warm to ferment for seven or eight days, stirring daily. Having done this, strain the wine through three or four thicknesses of muslin and wring out tightly. Clean the fermenting vessel and return the strained wine to this. Cover again as before and leave to ferment for a further three or four days. Then pour carefully into a warmed gallon jar, leaving as much deposit in the pail as you can. If the jar is not filled to where the neck begins, fill to this level with boiled cooled water. Then fit a fermentation lock and leave until all fermentation has ceased.

Damson Wines

Dry. 5 lb. damsons, ($\frac{3}{4}$ pt. Rosé concentrate), $2\frac{1}{2}$ lb. sugar, ($1\frac{3}{4}$ lb. sugar), all-purpose wine yeast, nutrient, $\frac{1}{2}$ level teaspoonful Pectinol, water as in method.

Sweet. 6 lb. damsons, ($\frac{3}{4}$ pt. Rosé concentrate), 3 lb. sugar, ($2\frac{1}{4}$ lb. sugar), all-purpose wine yeast, nutrient, $\frac{1}{2}$ level teaspoonful Pectinol, water as in method.

Remove stalks and rinse the damsons under a fast running tap. Put them in a saucepan with enough water to cover them, bring slowly to the boil and simmer gently until nearly cooled. Put the sugar in the fermenting vessel and pour the boiling damsons over this, stirring until the sugar is dissolved. Then make up to about five quarts with boiling water. Cover the mixture well and leave until lukewarm. Then crush half a Campden fruit preserving tablet to a powder and dissolve this in about a cupful of the juice and then mix into the bulk. Give the mixture a thorough stirring and stir in the concentrate if being used. Having done this, stir in the yeast, nutrient and Pectinol. Cover the vessel as advised, leave in the warm to ferment for five days, stirring daily. Then strain out the pulp through three or four thicknesses of muslin and wring out tightly. Clean the fermenting vessel and return the strained wine to this. Cover as before and leave to ferment for a further four or five days. The next step is to pour carefully into a warmed gallon jar leaving as much deposit in the pail as you can. If the jar is not filled to where the neck begins, fill to this level with boiled cooled water, then fit a fermentation lock and leave until all fermentation has ceased.

Plum Wines

Dry. 5 lb. plums, (1 pt. red concentrate), $2\frac{1}{2}$ lb. sugar, ($1\frac{1}{2}$ lb. sugar), all-purpose wine yeast, nutrient, $\frac{1}{2}$ level teaspoonful Pectinol, water as in method.

Sweet. 5 lb. plums, (1 pt. red concentrate), 3 lb. sugar, ($2\frac{1}{2}$ lb. sugar), all-purpose wine yeast, nutrient, $\frac{1}{2}$ level teaspoonful Pectinol, water as in method.

Remove stalks and rinse the plums under a fast running tap. Put them in a saucepan with enough water to cover them, bring them slowly to the boil and simmer until nearly cooked. Put the sugar in the fermenting pail and pour on the boiling plums, stirring until the sugar is dissolved. Then make up to five quarts with boiling water. Cover the mixture well and leave till lukewarm. Then crush half a Campden fruit preserving tablet to a powder and dissolve this in about a cupful of the juice and mix it into the bulk. Give the mixture a thorough stirring and then stir in the concentrate if being used. The next step is to stir in the yeast, nutrient and Pectinol. Cover the vessel as advised and leave in the warm to ferment for six or seven days, stirring daily. Then strain out the pulp through three or four thicknesses of muslin and wring out tightly. Clean the fermenting pail and return the strained wine to this. Cover as before and leave to ferment for a further three or four days. Then pour carefully into a warmed gallon jar, leaving as much deposit in the pail as you can. If the jar is not filled to where the neck begins, fill to this level with boiled cooled water, then fit a fermentation lock and leave until all fermentation has ceased.

Elderberry Wines

Dry. 3 lb. elderberries, ($\frac{3}{4}$ pt. Burgundy concentrate), $2\frac{1}{2}$ lb. sugar, ($1\frac{3}{4}$ lb. sugar), all-purpose wine yeast, nutrient, $\frac{1}{2}$ level teaspoonful Pectinol, water as in method.

Sweet. 4 lb. elderberries, ($\frac{3}{4}$ pt. Burgundy concentrate), 3 lb. sugar, ($2\frac{1}{4}$ lb. sugar), all-purpose wine yeast, nutrient, $\frac{1}{2}$ level teaspoonful Pectinol, water as in method.

Strip berries from the stalks (a large fork is useful for this). Do not use any red or green berries. Rinse the berries under a fast running tap, put them in a saucepan with enough water to cover them, bring slowly to the boil and simmer gently until broken. Put the sugar in the fermenting pail. Tie two or three thicknesses of muslin to the vessel so that it covers the top and leave a little depression by allowing the middle to sag. Place a loose cloth over this and pour the boiling berries into the sagging cloth carefully. Allow to drain for a while and then lift off the loose cloth containing the berries. Wring this out as tightly as possible over the tied-down muslin so that it acts as a second strainer. Having done this, remove the tied-down material, stir the juice until the sugar is dissolved and make up to one gallon with boiling water. Allow the mixture to cool to lukewarm. Crush half a Campden fruit preserving tablet to a powder and dissolve this in about a cupful of the juice and stir it into the bulk. Having done this, stir in the concentrate if being used, then stir in the yeast, nutrient and Pectinol. Cover the vessel as advised and leave in the warm to ferment for seven or eight days, stirring daily. The next step is to pour carefully into a gallon jar leaving as much deposit in the pail as you can. If the jar is not filled to where the neck begins, fill to this level with boiled cooled water, then fit a fermentation lock and leave until all fermentation has ceased.

Peach Wines

Dry. 3½ lb. peaches, (½ pt. Hock or Rosé concentrate), 2¼ lb.
sugar, (1¾ lb. sugar), all-purpose wine yeast, nutrient, ½ level
teaspoonful Pectinol, water as in method.
Sweet. 4 lb. peaches (¾ pt. Hock or Rosé concentrate), 3 lb.
sugar, (2¼ lb. sugar), all-purpose wine yeast, nutrient, ½ level
teaspoonful Pectinol, water as in method.

Halve the peaches, remove the stones and peel them. Put
the fruit in a saucepan with enough water to cover well, bring
slowly to the boil and simmer until tender or nearly cooked.
Put the sugar in the fermenting pail and pour on the boiling
fruits, stirring until the sugar is dissolved. Then make up to
about nine pints with boiling water. Having done this, allow
the mixture to cool to lukewarm. Crush half a Campden fruit
preserving tablet to a powder, dissolve this in about a cupful
of the juice and stir it into the bulk. Stir in the concentrate if
being used, and either way, give the mixture a thorough
stirring. Then stir in the yeast, nutrient and Pectinol. Cover
the vessel as advised and leave in the warm to ferment for
seven or eight days, stirring daily. The next step is to strain
the wine through three or four thicknesses of muslin and to
wring out the pulp as dry as you can. Return the strained
wine to the fermenting pail, previously cleaned, cover as
before and leave for a further three or four days. Then pour
carefully into a gallon jar leaving as much deposit in the pail
as you can. If the jar is not filled to where the neck begins, fill
to this level with boiled cooled water, then fit a fermentation
lock and leave until all fermentation has ceased.

Apricot Wines

Follow exactly the recipes and method for peach wines.

Ten

Making Fruit Wines by the Sulphiting Method

This method will always be popular, not only because it is simple and quick, but also because of the flavours of the wines made by it. These flavours are more or less of the fresh uncooked fruits, but these are naturally changed to some extent by the process of fermentation. Do bear in mind however that the flavours of fruit wines made by this method are quite different from those made by the heat treatment method in the previous chapter.

In my more than thirty years of wine-making I must have made nearly every type of wine by many different methods and I still cannot say with certainty which method is the best, for the very simple reason that each method makes for a different type of flavour and a different type of wine, and all are excellent. Indeed, I prefer my home-made wines to commercial products. The only commercial wines I buy are the better sherries.

Some overseas visitors staying with me during the summer sampled quite a few of my wines, Their comments delighted me and summed up the whole situation of experienced amateur wine-making perfectly: 'But you cannot even *buy* wines like these.' – meaning that there is not a commercial wine to compare with them. Well, I'm not going to try to qualify that – except to say that very many commercial wines which have become popular for some reason are thin, lacking in flavour and nearly always a little too acid for my liking. But there it is, and always will be – a matter of taste. I think this is the reason for many people suggesting as much as two teaspoonfuls of citric acid as being the ideal for even a fruit wine recipe which would have the fruit's natural acid content as well. They are trying to emulate the over-acid wines from the continent. The reason I avoid recommending acid in recipes for fruit wines is that I know, despite my exhortations to use only ripe fruits, that everybody lets a few unripe ones into the must. The higher acid content of the unripe ones together with the lower acid content of the ripe ones brings the overall acid content of the must, and therefore the wine, up to a palatable level.

It will be seen that in this chapter I give three recipes for each fruit – one for dry wine, one for medium and one for sweet – and the wines should turn out as planned if fermentation is as satisfactory as it should be. A medium dry to medium sweet wine is always difficult to achieve with certainty because we add just enough sugar to overcome the dryness and not enough to produce a sweet wine. But – and it is a big but – if fermentation happened to be better than average, a rather drier wine than a medium would result because the better than average fermentation would use up more sugar, produce more alcohol and therefore produce a drier than expected wine. Conversely, if fermentation happened to be not quite up to expectations, less sugar would be used up with the result that what should have been a medium-dry-to-medium-sweet, might turn out to be a sweet wine.

Much would depend on your conception of dryness and sweetness. What is dry to one person is almost sweet to another. What is dry to another person is much too dry for others. Similarly, what is pleasantly sweet to one person is often quite sickly sweet to another. So you will now appreciate the difficulty that a bloke like me has in trying to give you what you want! If you are not sure whether you like dry wines buy a bottle of Beaujolais or a dry Rosé, sample them and you will know at once whether dry wines are for you. Similarly, if you are not sure whether you like the fully sweet wines, sample one of the sweet Sauternes. Testing your palate in this way will save you making the type of wines you wish you had not.

However, if all works out as it should, the type of wine

aimed at should result readily enough. The three recipes for each fruit are followed immediately by one method which is suitable for all the recipes for that particular fruit. So all you have to do is to select the recipe you want to use – dry, medium or sweet – and then use the method following. This will either be on the same page or on the one immediately after, so you cannot go wrong. Using this method to present to you the recipes and methods allows me much more space to give for more recipes and methods than would be possible if I had to write out a fully detailed method for each recipe. It will be seen in the recipes that I include the addition of a certain amount of concentrated grape juice. The amount and type to use is set in brackets. A second amount of sugar is also set in brackets. If you do not want to use the grape juice, do not do so. If you do not, then also ignore the second amount of sugar, in brackets. In other words, ignore both items in brackets and work with the basic ingredients. The wines resulting from these will be very good wines. *Note*: The sugar in concentrated grape juices settles to the bottom of the can. To dissolve this so that it may be dispersed before use, open the can, stand it in a saucepan of hot water and after a few minutes stir until the sugar is dissolved. When using the concentrate, measure out the amount required, put the remainder in such as a small Kilner jar, screw on the lid tightly and use for a new batch of wine as soon as you can.

Important Note: It will be seen in the methods that I give the instruction 'stir in the syrup'. It will also be seen that I suggest boiled water that has cooled. Obviously a gallon of boiled water takes a long time to cool, so does sugar syrup. Therefore, before you begin to prepare the other ingredients, boil one gallon of water say six or seven hours before you make the wine. Similarly, it is wise to see how much sugar is needed by consulting the recipe you propose to use, and to put this in a saucepan with about a quart of water, bring it slowly to the boil stirring very frequently to prevent it settling and perhaps burning on to the bottom of the saucepan. When it has boiled, put the lid on and let it cool naturally. If it happens to be a little too cold when required for use, a few minutes over heat will make it easier to disperse into the must.

Loganberry Wines (Rosé types)

Dry. 4 lb. loganberries, ($\frac{3}{4}$ pt. Rosé concentrate), $2\frac{1}{4}$ lb. sugar, ($1\frac{1}{2}$ lb. sugar), all-purpose wine yeast, nutrient, $\frac{1}{2}$ level teaspoonful Pectinol, water as in method.

Medium. 4 lb. loganberries, ($\frac{3}{4}$ pt. Rosé concentrate), $2\frac{1}{4}$ lb. sugar, (2 lb. sugar), all-purpose wine yeast, nutrient, $\frac{1}{2}$ level teaspoonful Pectinol, water as in method.

Sweet. 4 to 5 lb. loganberries, ($\frac{3}{4}$ pt. Rosé concentrate), 3 lb. sugar, ($2\frac{1}{4}$ lb. sugar), all-purpose wine yeast, nutrient, $\frac{1}{2}$ level teaspoonful Pectinol, water as in method.

Hull loganberries, rinse them under a fast running tap, put them in the fermenting pail and crush well by hand, and then stir in half a gallon of boiled cooled water. Crush one Campden fruit preserving tablet to a powder, dissolve this well in about half a cupful of warm water and then stir it into the pulp. Add the concentrate if being used and stir this in. Stir in the syrup. Having done this make up to about a gallon and a quart with boiled cooled water. The next step is to give the whole lot a thorough stirring and then add the yeast, nutrient and Pectinol.

Having done this, cover as advised and put in the warm to ferment for seven days, stirring daily. After this, strain the wines through several thicknesses of muslin, wring out the pulp as dry as you can and return the strained wine to the cleaned fermenting pail. Cover again as before and leave to ferment for a further three or four days. Then pour carefully into a warmed gallon jar, leaving as much deposit in the pail as you can. If the jar is not filled to where the neck begins, fill to this level with boiled cooled water, then fit a fermentation lock and leave until all fermentation has ceased.

Blackcurrant Wines (Burgundy styles)

Dry. 3 lb. blackcurrants, ($\frac{1}{2}$ pt. Burgundy concentrate), $2\frac{1}{4}$ lb. sugar, ($1\frac{3}{4}$ lb. sugar), all-purpose wine yeast, nutrient, $\frac{1}{2}$ level teaspoonful Pectinol, water as in method.

1 Gallon = 8 pints

Medium. 3 lb. blackcurrants, (¾ pt. Burgundy concentrate), 2¾ lb. sugar, (2 lb. sugar), all-purpose wine yeast, nutrient, ½ level teaspoonful Pectinol, water as in method.

Sweet. 3 to 3½ lb. blackcurrants, (¾ pt. Burgundy concentrate), 3 lb. sugar, (2¼ lb. sugar), all-purpose wine yeast, nutrient, ½ level teaspoonful Pectinol, water as in method.

Remove stalks and rinse the fruits under a fast running tap. Put them in the fermenting pail and crush well by hand, and then stir in about half a gallon of boiled cooled water. Crush one Campden fruit preserving tablet in about a cupful of warm water and stir this into the pulp. Add the concentrate if being used and stir this in. Stir in the syrup. Having done this make up this mixture to about a gallon and a quart with boiled water that has cooled. Then give the mixture a thorough churning up. After this, add the yeast, nutrient and Pectinol.

The next step is to cover the vessel as advised and keep the mixture in the warm to ferment for seven days, stirring daily. Then strain the wine through several thicknesses of muslin, wring out the pulp as dry as you can and return the strained wine to the cleaned fermenting pail. Cover again as before and leave in the warm to ferment for a further three or four days. Having done this, pour the wine carefully into a warmed gallon jar leaving as much deposit in the pail as possible. If the jar is not filled to where the neck begins, fill to this level with boiled cooled water, then fit a fermentation lock and leave until all fermentation has ceased.

Redcurrant Wines

Follow exactly the recipes and method for blackcurrant wines, using a Rosé concentrate (if desired).

Whitecurrant Wines

Follow exactly the recipes and method for blackcurrant wines, using a Hock concentrate (if desired).

Gooseberry Wines

Dry. 4 lb. gooseberries, ($\frac{1}{2}$ pt. Hock concentrate), $2\frac{1}{4}$ lb. sugar, ($1\frac{3}{4}$ lb. sugar), all-purpose wine yeast, nutrient, $\frac{1}{2}$ level teaspoonful Pectinol, water as in method.

Medium. 4 lb. gooseberries, ($\frac{1}{2}$ pt. Hock concentrate), $2\frac{3}{4}$ lb. sugar, ($2\frac{1}{4}$ lb. sugar), all-purpose wine yeast, nutrient, $\frac{1}{2}$ level teaspoonful Pectinol, water as in method.

Sweet. 5 lb. gooseberries, ($\frac{3}{4}$ pt. Hock concentrate), 3 lb. sugar, ($2\frac{1}{4}$ lb. sugar), all-purpose wine yeast, nutrient, $\frac{1}{2}$ level teaspoonful Pectinol, water as in method.

Top and tail the gooseberries, rinse them under a fast-running tap, put them in the fermenting pail and crush well by hand. Then mix them well with about half a gallon of boiled cooled water. Crush one Campden fruit preserving tablet to a powder and dissolve this in about a cupful of warm water, then stir this into the must, and stir in the concentrate if being used. Stir in the syrup. Having done this, make up the mixture to about five quarts with boiled cooled water. Then give the mixture a thorough stirring. Having done this, add the yeast, nutrient and Pectinol. Cover the vessel as advised and keep in the warm to ferment for seven days stirring daily. After this, strain through several thicknesses of muslin and return the strained wine to the cleaned fermenting pail. Cover as before and leave in the warm to ferment for a further three or four days. Then pour carefully into a warmed gallon jar leaving as much deposit in the pail as you can. If the jar is not filled to where the neck begins, fill to this level with boiled cooled water, then fit a fermentation lock and leave until all fermentation has ceased.

Blackberry Wines (Beaujolais and Burgundy styles)

Dry. Beaujolais style. 4 lb. blackberries, ($\frac{3}{4}$ pt. Burgundy concentrate), 2 lb. sugar, ($1\frac{3}{4}$ lb. sugar), all-purpose wine yeast, nutrient, $\frac{1}{2}$ level teaspoonful Pectinol, water as in method.

Medium. Burgundy style. 4 lb. blackberries, ($\frac{3}{4}$ pt. Burgundy concentrate), $2\frac{3}{4}$ lb. sugar, (2 lb. sugar), all-purpose wine yeast, nutrient, $\frac{1}{2}$ level teaspoonful Pectinol, water as in method.

Sweet. Burgundy style. 4 to 5 lb. blackberries, (1 pt. Burgundy concentrate), 3 lb. sugar, (2 lb. sugar), all-purpose wine yeast, nutrient, $\frac{1}{2}$ level teaspoonful Pectinol, water as in method.

Remove stalks, rinse the fruits under a fast running tap, put them in the fermenting pail and crush well by hand, then stir in about half a gallon of boiled cooled water. Crush one Campden fruit preserving tablet to a powder and dissolve this in about a cupful of warm water and stir into the mixture. Stir in the concentrate if being used. Stir in the syrup. Having done this make up the mixture to about five quarts with boiled cooled water. Then give the mixture a thorough stirring. Having done this, add the yeast, nutrient and Pectinol. Cover the vessel as advised and keep the mixture in the warm to ferment for seven or eight days, stirring daily. After this, strain through several thicknesses of muslin, wring out the pulp as dry as you can and return the strained wine to the cleaned fermenting vessel. Cover this as before and leave to ferment for a further three or four days.

The next step is to pour the wine into a warmed gallon jar leaving as much deposit in the pail as you can. If the jar is not filled to where the neck begins, fill to this level with boiled cooled water. Then fit a fermentation lock and leave until all fermentation has ceased.

Damson Wines (Full-flavoured robust Rosé types)

Dry. 4 lb. damsons, ($\frac{3}{4}$ lb. Rosé concentrate), $2\frac{1}{4}$ lb. sugar, ($1\frac{1}{2}$ lb. sugar), all-purpose wine yeast, nutrient, $\frac{1}{2}$ level teaspoonful Pectinol, water as in method.

Medium. 5 lb. damsons, ($\frac{3}{4}$ pt. Rosé concentrate), $2\frac{3}{4}$ lb. sugar, (2 lb. sugar), all-purpose wine yeast, nutrient, $\frac{1}{2}$ level teaspoonful Pectinol, water as in method.

Sweet. 6 to 7 lb. damsons, (1 pt. Rosé concentrate), 3 lb. sugar, (2 lb. sugar), all-purpose wine yeast, nutrient, $\frac{1}{2}$ level teaspoonful Pectinol, water as in method.

Remove stalks, rinse the fruits under a fast running tap, put them in the fermenting vessel and crush well by hand. Then mix in about half a gallon of boiled cooled water. Crush one ($1\frac{1}{2}$ if 6-7 lb. fruit is used), Campden fruit preserving tablet to a powder and dissolve this in about a cupful of warm water, and stir into the must. Stir in the concentrate if being used. Stir in the syrup. Having done this, make the mixture up to about five quarts with boiled cooled water. Then give the mixture a thorough stirring. The next step is to add the yeast, nutrient and Pectinol. Cover the vessel as advised and keep the mixture in the warm to ferment for seven days – not longer – stirring daily. After this, strain the must through three or four thicknesses of muslin, wring out the pulp as dry as you can and return the strained wine to the cleaned fermenting vessel. Cover as before and leave in the warm to ferment for a further three or four days.

The next step is to pour the wine into a warmed gallon jar leaving as much deposit in the pail as you can. If the jar is not filled to where the neck begins, fill to this level with boiled cooled water, then fit a fermentation lock and leave until all fermentation has ceased.

Plum Wines (Burgundy and Port style)

Dry. Burgundy style. 5 lb. black plums, (1 pt. Burgundy concentrate), $2\frac{1}{4}$ lb. sugar, ($1\frac{1}{4}$ lb. sugar), all-purpose wine yeast, nutrient, $\frac{1}{2}$ level teaspoonful Pectinol, water as in method.

Medium. Burgundy style. 6 lb. black plums, (1 pt. Burgundy concentrate), $2\frac{3}{4}$ lb. sugar, ($1\frac{3}{4}$ lb. sugar), all-purpose wine yeast, nutrient, $\frac{1}{2}$ level teaspoonful Pectinol, water as in method.

Sweet. Port style. 6 or 7 lb. black plums, (1 pt. Port or Ruby concentrate), 3 lb. sugar, (2 lb. sugar), all-purpose wine yeast, nutrient, $\frac{1}{2}$ level teaspoonful Pectinol, water as in method.

Remove stalks, rinse fruit under a fast running tap, put them in the fermenting pail and crush well by hand. Then mix in about half a gallon of boiled cooled water. Crush one (1½ for 6-7 lb. fruit) Campden fruit preserving tablet to a powder and dissolve this in about a cupful of warm water, and stir it into the must. Stir in the concentrate if being used and then give the mixture a thorough stirring. Stir in the syrup. Having done this make up the mixture to about five quarts with boiled cooled water. The next step is to add the yeast, nutrient and Pectinol. Then cover the vessel as advised and put in the warm to ferment for seven or eight days, stirring daily. After this, strain the must through three or four thicknesses of muslin and wring out as dry as you can. Return the strained wine to the cleaned fermenting vesel, cover as before and leave in the warm to ferment for a further three or four days.

The next step is to pour carefully into a warmed gallon jar, leaving as much deposit in the pail as you can. If the jar is not filled to where the neck begins, fill to this level with boiled cooled water, then fit a fermentation lock and leave until all fermentation has ceased.

Elderberry Wines (Burgundy and Port styles)

Dry. Burgundy style. 3 lb. elderberries, (¾ pt. Burgundy concentrate), 2¼ lb. sugar, (1½ lb. sugar), all-purpose wine yeast, nutrient, ½ level teaspoonful Pectinol, water as in method.

Medium. Burgundy – Port style. 3 lb. elderberries, (¾ pt. Burgundy or Port concentrate), 2¾ lb. sugar, (2 lb. sugar), all-purpose wine yeast, nutrient, ½ level teaspoonful Pectinol, water as in method.

Sweet. Port style. 4 lb. elderberries, (1 pt. Port concentrate), 3 lb. sugar, (2 lb. sugar), all-purpose wine yeast, nutrient, ½ level teaspoonful Pectinol, water as in method.

Strip berries from stalks, rinse them under a fast running tap, put them in the fermenting vessel and crush well by hand. Then mix in about half a gallon of boiled cooled water. Crush one Campden fruit preserving tablet to a powder and dissolve this in about a cupful of warm water, and stir it into the pulp. Stir in the concentrate if being used and give the mixture a thorough stirring. Stir in the syrup. Having done this make up the mixture to about five quarts with boiled cooled water. Stir well again, then stir in the yeast, nutrient and Pectinol. Cover the vessel as advised and ferment in a warm place for three or four days – not longer. The next step is to strain the wine through three or four thicknesses of muslin and press out all the juice, but do not wring out dry. Clean the fermenting vessel and return the strained wine to this. Cover as before and leave in the warm to ferment for a further seven or eight days. Then pour carefully into a warmed gallon jar, leaving as much deposit in the pail as you can. If the jar is not filled to where the neck begins, fill to this level with boiled cooled water, then fit a fermentation lock and leave until all fermentation has ceased.

Peach Wines

Dry. 4 lb. peaches, ($\frac{1}{2}$ pt. Hock concentrate), $2\frac{3}{4}$ lb. sugar, ($1\frac{3}{4}$ lb. sugar), all-purpose wine yeast, nutrient, $\frac{1}{2}$ level teaspoonful Pectinol, water as in method.

Medium. 5 lb. peaches, ($\frac{3}{4}$ pt. Hock concentrate), $2\frac{3}{4}$ lb. sugar, (2 lb. sugar), all-purpose wine yeast, nutrient, $\frac{1}{2}$ level teaspoonful Pectinol, water as in method.

Sweet. 5 to 6 lb. peaches, ($\frac{3}{4}$ lb. Hock concentrate), 3 lb. sugar, ($2\frac{1}{4}$ lb. sugar), all-purpose wine yeast, nutrient, $\frac{1}{2}$ level teaspoonful Pectinol, water as in method.

Halve the peaches, remove the stones and peel them. Put the fruits in the fermenting vessel and crush well by hand. Then mix in about half a gallon of boiled cooled water. Crush one Campden fruit preserving tablet to a powder, dissolve this in about a cupful of warm water and stir it into the must. Stir in the concentrate if being used and give the mixture a thorough stirring. Stir in the syrup. Having done this, make up the mixture to about five quarts with boiled cooled water, then give another vigorous stirring. The next step is to add the yeast, nutrient and Pectinol. Cover the vessel as advised and leave in a warm place to ferment for six or seven days, stirring daily. The next step is to strain the wine through three or four thicknesses of muslin and to wring out the pulp as dry as you can. Clean the fermenting vessel and return the strained wine to this. Cover as before and leave in the warm to ferment for a further three or four days. After this, pour carefully into a warmed gallon jar leaving as much deposit in the pail as you can. If the jar is not filled to where the neck begins, fill to this level with boiled cooled water, then fit a fermentation lock and leave until all fermentation has ceased.

Apricot Wines

Follow exactly the recipes and methods for Peach wines.

Rhubarb Wines

Rhubarb – especially if you happen to grow it yourself – is a cheap and plentiful basic ingredient for making a wide variety of wines. You can make a Rosé or an imitation Riesling by combining it with other fruits. This aspect is covered in a later chapter. I concern myself here with combining it with concentrated grape juice. The dry and medium will be aperitif types while the sweet will be more in line with a dessert type. These will be slightly on the acid side owing to the presence of oxalic acid in the rhubarb. Do not worry about this. Many people believe that to drink rhubarb wine can be harmful because oxalic acid is mildly poisonous. The fact is that you would have to drink several gallons at one sitting for it to have any harmful effects and I hate to think what effect the alcohol would have had in that time. Indeed, you cannot drink enough rhubarb wine for the acid to harm you without taking a terrific clobbering from the alcohol content first. I and many friends as well as hundreds of thousands of people all over the country make and drink their rhubarb wine without ill effects. There is most likely more oxalic acid in a small rhubarb pie or dish of stewed rhubarb than there is in a bottle of rhubarb wine and nobody gets hurt by eating stewed rhubarb or rhubarb pie.

Dry. 3 lb. rhubarb, ($\frac{1}{2}$ pt. Hock concentrate), $2\frac{1}{4}$ lb. sugar, ($1\frac{3}{4}$ lb. sugar), all-purpose wine yeast, nutrient, $\frac{1}{2}$ level teaspoonful Pectinol, water as in method.

Medium. 3 lb. rhubarb, ($\frac{1}{2}$ pt. Hock concentrate), $2\frac{3}{4}$ lb. sugar, ($2\frac{1}{4}$ lb. sugar), all-purpose wine yeast, nutrient, $\frac{1}{2}$ level teaspoonful Pectinol, water as in method.

Sweet (A sweet wine with an underlying acidity) 4 lb. rhubarb, ($\frac{3}{4}$ pt. Hock concentrate), 3 lb. sugar, ($2\frac{1}{4}$ lb. sugar), all-purpose wine yeast, nutrient, $\frac{1}{2}$ level teaspoonful Pectinol, water as in method.

Remove stumps and leaves and wipe the sticks clean with a damp cloth. Cut them into short lengths and crush with a rolling pin, being careful not to lose any juice. Put the juice and pulp in the fermenting pail and mix in about half a gallon of boiled cooled water. Crush one Campden fruit preserving tablet to a powder, dissolve this in about a cupful of warm water and stir it into the must. Stir in the concentrate if being used and give the must a thorough stirring. Having done this, stir in the syrup, giving the mixture another good stirring. Then add the yeast, nutrient and Pectinol. Cover as advised, and put the mixture in a warm place to ferment for seven or eight days, stirring daily. The next step is to strain the wine through three or four thicknesses of muslin and to wring out the pulp as dry as you can. Clean the fermenting vessel and return the strained wine to this. Cover as before and leave to ferment for a further three or four days. After this, pour carefully into a warmed gallon jar, leaving as much deposit in the pail as you can. If the jar is not filled to where the neck begins, fill to this level with boiled cooled water, then fit a fermentation lock and leave until all fermentation has ceased.

Cherry Wines (Delightful fruity Rosé, or dessert types)

Dry. 5 lb. black cherries, ($\frac{1}{2}$ pt. Rosé concentrate), $2\frac{1}{4}$ lb. sugar, $1\frac{3}{4}$ lb. sugar), all-purpose wine yeast, nutrient, $\frac{1}{2}$ level teaspoonful Pectinol, water as in method.

Medium. 5 lb. black cherries, ($\frac{1}{2}$ pt. Ruby concentrate), $2\frac{3}{4}$ lb. sugar, ($2\frac{1}{4}$ lb. sugar), all-purpose wine yeast, nutrient, $\frac{1}{2}$ level teaspoonful Pectinol, water as in method.

Sweet. 6 lb. black cherries, ($\frac{3}{4}$ pt. Ruby concentrate), 3 lb. sugar, ($2\frac{1}{4}$ lb. sugar), all-purpose wine yeast, nutrient, $\frac{1}{2}$ level teaspoonful Pectinol, water as in method.

Remove stalks, rinse the cherries under a fast running tap, put them in a fermenting vessel and crush them well by hand, (don't worry about the stones) and then mix in about half a gallon of boiled cooled water. Crush one Campden fruit preserving tablet to powder, dissolve this in about a cupful of warm water and stir into the pulp. Stir in the concentrate if being used and give the mixture a thorough stirring. Having done this, stir in the syrup and give the mixture another stirring. Then make up to about five quarts with boiled cooled water. The next step is to add the yeast, nutrient and Pectinol. After this, cover as advised and leave the must in the warm to ferment for seven or eight days, stirring daily. Then strain the wine through three or four thicknesses of muslin and wring out the pulp as dry as you can. Clean the fermenting vessel and return the strained wine to this. Cover as before and leave in the warm to ferment for a further three or four days. Then pour carefully into a warmed gallon jar, leaving as much deposit in the pail as you can. If the jar is not filled to where the neck begins, fill to this level with boiled cooled water, then fit a fermentation lock and leave until all fermentation has ceased.

Eleven

Special Recipes

I first published a wide range of recipes for using mixtures of ingredients back in 1966. The book has become extremely popular here as well as in Canada, USA, Australia and New Zealand. This great success prompted me to carry out further trials and experiments in order to find an even wider range of varied ingredients and so produce recipes which would produce a far wider range of wine types. And I must confess that while some of the results were not up to expectations, others made some very exceptional wines. There is no end to the variety of combinations of ingredients that may be used, so if you happen to be of an experimental turn of mind you will when you have used some of these recipes be able to judge for yourself how you may slightly alter a recipe to include a little additional fruit of some other variety and so evolve a new recipe. All that need be borne in mind is that if you use additional or a different dried fruit you must allow for its sugar content. Bear in mind that the sugar contained in dried fruits does not register on the hydrometer if the specific gravity is taken just before the commencement of fermentation simply because it is not distributed throughout as soluble sugar. Instead, it is distributed throughout the must somewhat gradually. Chopping or mincing dried fruits will speed up the distribution of their sugar content. But in the early stages you would obtain a misleading specific gravity reading if you happen to take it.

Elderberries, bilberries and sloes are the exception, otherwise most other dried fruit contain approximately 50 per cent sugar – one pound of raisins, for example, contains approximately $\frac{1}{2}$ lb. of sugar.

This fact is allowed for in the recipes, so there is no need for you to make calculations as to the amount of sugar required.

It will be noted that very small amounts of certain dried fruits are recommended in the following recipes. This is because they have a pronounced flavour and because one pound of the dried product is the approximate equivalent to four pounds of the fresh fruit. It will also be seen that the recipes are numbered. The method to use with the recipe will be found on the page indicated in the recipe.

The description of the type of wine the recipe will make, Rosé, Burgundy, etc., is there as a guide. These wine types will be quite different to the types made in other chapters, nevertheless, they will make excellent Rosé or Burgundy types as the case may be, in the same way that commercial products vary with each producer. (The 5 ml. spoon used is, as you will have guessed, the spoon issued with medical prescriptions.)

Recipe No. 1   Bilberry Rosé style

$\frac{1}{2}$ lb. dried bilberries, 1 lb. sultanas, 2 level 5 ml. spoonfuls citric acid, all-purpose wine yeast, nutrient, $\frac{1}{2}$ level teaspoonful Pectinol, sugar: for dry 1$\frac{1}{2}$ lb., for medium 2$\frac{1}{4}$ lb., water as in method on page 88.

Recipe No 2   Bilberry Burgundy style

$\frac{1}{2}$ lb. dried bilberries, 1 lb. sultanas, 1 lb. fresh or tinned blackberries, 2 level 5 ml. spoonfuls citric acid, all-purpose wine yeast, nutrient, $\frac{1}{2}$ level teaspoonful Pectinol, sugar: for dry 1$\frac{1}{2}$ lb., for medium 2$\frac{1}{4}$ lb., water as in method on page 88.

Recipe No. 3   Bilberry Burgundy style – (sweet)

As above using 2$\frac{3}{4}$ lb. sugar and 2$\frac{1}{4}$ level 5 ml. spoonfuls citric acid instead of the amounts stated.

Recipe No. 4   Elderberry Burgundy style

$\frac{1}{2}$ lb. dried elderberries, 1 lb. sultanas, 1 lb. damsons fresh or tinned, 2 level 5 ml. spoonfuls citric acid, all-purpose wine yeast, nutrient, $\frac{1}{2}$ level teaspoonful Pectinol, sugar: for dry $1\frac{1}{2}$ lb., for medium $1\frac{3}{4}$ lb., water as in method on page 88.

Recipe No. 5   Elderberry Port style

$\frac{1}{4}$ lb. dried elderberries, $\frac{1}{2}$ lb. dried bilberries, 1 lb. fresh or tinned blackberries, 1 lb. sultanas, 2 level 5 ml. spoonfuls citric acid, all-purpose wine yeast, nutrient, $\frac{1}{2}$ level teaspoonful Pectinol, sugar: for medium $2\frac{1}{4}$ lb., for sweet $2\frac{1}{2}$ lb., water as in method on page 88.

Recipe No. 6   Elderberry/Bilberry Rosé

$\frac{1}{4}$ lb. dried elderberries, $\frac{1}{4}$ lb. dried bilberries, 1 lb. sultanas, 1 lb. fresh or tinned rhubarb, (NO acid), all-purpose wine yeast, nutrient, $\frac{1}{2}$ level teaspoonful Pectinol, sugar: for dry $1\frac{3}{4}$ lb., for medium $2\frac{1}{4}$ lb., water as in method on page 88.

Recipe No. 7   Dried Apricot Wine

1 lb. dried apricots, 1 lb. sultanas, $1\frac{1}{2}$ level 5 ml. spoonfuls citric acid, $\frac{1}{2}$ pt. strong tea, all-purpose wine yeast, nutrient, $\frac{1}{2}$ level teaspoonful Pectinol, sugar: for dry $1\frac{3}{4}$ lb., for medium $2\frac{1}{4}$ lb., for sweet $2\frac{1}{2}$ lb., water as in method on page 88.

Recipe No. 8   Dried Peach Wine

1 lb. dried peaches, $\frac{1}{2}$ lb. sultanas, $\frac{1}{2}$ lb. raisins, 2 level 5 ml. spoonfuls citric acid, $\frac{1}{2}$ pt. strong tea, all-purpose wine yeast, nutrient, $\frac{1}{2}$ level teaspoonful Pectinol, sugar: for dry $1\frac{3}{4}$ lb.,

for medium 2¼ lb., for sweet 2½ lb., water as in method on page 88.

Recipe No. 9   Dried Prune Wine

1½ lb. dried prunes, 1 lb. fresh or tinned blackberries, ½ lb. sultanas, 2 level 5 ml. spoonfuls citric acid, 1 pt. strong tea, all-purpose wine yeast, nutrient, ½ level teaspoonful Pectinol, sugar: for dry 1¼ lb., for medium 1¾ lb., for sweet 2¼ lb., water as in method on page 88. If making the sweet use ½ a 5 ml. spoonful of citric acid extra and ½ lb. more prunes.

Recipe No. 10   Dried Currant Wine

1 lb. dried currants, ½ lb. sultanas, 1 lb. fresh or tinned black-berries, 2 level 5 ml. spoonfuls citric acid, ½ pt. strong tea, all-purpose wine yeast, nutrient, ½ level teaspoonful Pectinol, sugar: for dry 2 lb., for medium 2¼ lb., for sweet 2½ lb., water as in method on page 88.

Recipe No. 11   Dried Currant and Loganberry Wine

1 lb. dried currants, ½ lb. raisins, 1½ lb. fresh or tinned logan-berries, 2 level 5 ml. spoonfuls citric acid, ½ pt. strong tea, all-purpose wine yeast, ½ level teaspoonful Pectinol, sugar: for dry 1¾ lb., for medium 2¼ lb., for sweet 2½ lb., water as in method on page 88.

Recipe No. 12   Fig Wine (Resembling Sherry)

1½ lb. dried figs (or ¾ pt. concentrated fig juice), 1 lb. raisins, 2 level 5 ml. spoonfuls citric acid, ½ pt. strong tea, all-purpose wine yeast, nutrient, ½ level teaspoonful Pectinol, sugar (use soft brown): for dry 1½ lb., for medium 1¾ lb., for sweet 2 lb., water as in method on page 88. When making this wine follow the method, but when fermentation has ceased, remove

the lock and bung, empty the lock and plug the open end
with cotton wool, return the lock and bung the jar tightly
and leave in a cool place for two weeks. Then bung down in
the usual way and keep for at least six months.

Recipe No. 13   Dried Sloe Wine

½ lb. dried sloes, ½ lb. sultanas, 1 lb. fresh or tinned red plums,
2 level 5 ml. spoonfuls citric acid, all-purpose wine yeast,
nutrient, ½ level teaspoonful Pectinol, sugar: for dry 2 lb.,
for medium 2½ lb., for sweet 2¾ lb., water as in method
below.

Recipe No. 14   Dried Sloe Rosé

½ lb. dried sloes, ½ lb. sultanas, 1 lb. fresh or tinned loganberries, 2 level 5 ml. spoonfuls citric acid, all-purpose wine
yeast, nutrient, ½ level teaspoonful Pectinol, sugar: for dry
2 lb., for medium 2½ lb., for sweet 3 lb., water as in method
below.

Method for Recipes 1 to 14

Before you begin, dried elderberries, sloes and bilberries
must be thoroughly washed under a fast running tap. Because
dried elderberries are so tiny it is sensible to line the colander
with fine muslin to prevent losing them. Other dried fruit,
having been thoroughly prepared and packeted, need not be
washed but should be finely chopped or minced before they
are put into the fermenting pail. Dried prunes are the exception, these should be stoned and cut up.

Put all the fruits called for in the recipe in the fermenting
pail. This includes concentrated fig juice if being used as in
recipe No. 12 and, of course, tinned fruits where being used.
Having done this pour over them about half a gallon of
boiling water. Put the sugar in a saucepan with about a quart
of water, bring it slowly to the boil stirring frequently and

then pour this into the rest and stir well. Then make up the mixture to about five quarts with boiling water. Allow the mixture to cool to lukewarm, then crush half a Campden fruit preserving tablet to a powder and dissolve this in about half a cupful of warm water. Stir this into the mixture and then give it a thorough churning. The next step is to add the tea and acid where required in the recipe and to add the yeast and nutrient. Cover the vessel as advised and keep it in the warm to ferment for eight or nine days, stirring daily – but only five days where dried elderberries, sloes or bilberries are being used. Having done this, strain the mixture through three or four thicknesses of muslin and wring out the pulp as dry as you can. Clean the fermenting pail and return the strained wine to this. Cover as before and keep the wine in the warm to continue fermenting for a further three or four days – but six or seven days where dried elderberries, sloes or bilberries are being used.

After the required time in the fermenting pail, pour the wine carefully into a warmed one-gallon jar leaving as much deposit in the pail as you can and then stir in the Pectinol. If the jar is not filled to where the neck begins, fill to the level with boiled cooled water, then fit a fermentation lock and leave until all fermentation has ceased.

Twelve

Rhubarb Wines

As I said earlier, rhubarb is a cheap and plentiful basic ingredient – especially if you grow it yourself. If you do not, it is a good plan to get a couple of crowns in February and to plant them in deeply-dug soil that has had time to settle. In a year or so, you will have more rhubarb that you can use for wine-making. Rhubarb is a versatile ingredient in that it will blend its flavour with a wide variety of fruits (rhubarb being a vegetable) without obliterating the flavours of the fruits used in making the wines. You will, of course, still have the flavour of rhubarb in the background of any wine made with the recipes here, but this is not a bad thing. Wines containing the flavour of rhubarb are always best dry-to-medium. But this does not mean that they cannot be made sweet if you want them that way. After all, many people cannot tolerate a medium or dry wine, so you may decide for yourself whether to make them dry, medium or sweet.

With its characteristic flavour it is almost impossible to imitate commercial products when using rhubarb alone, but with additional ingredients this is not too difficult. You will see that I give at the head of each recipe an indication of the type of wine the recipe will make. Bear in mind that if I mention Rosé more than once it is because the fruit used with the basic ingredient (rhubarb) will be responsible for producing the differently flavoured Rosé.

Rhubarb Wine (Riesling style)

1½ lb. rhubarb, 1 lb. sultanas, 2 grapefruit (large), all-purpose wine yeast, nutrient, ½ level teaspoonful Pectinol, sugar: for dry 2 lb., for medium 2¼ lb., for sweet 2½ lb., water as in method on page 92.

Rhubarb Wine (Light claret style)

2 lb. rhubarb, $\frac{1}{2}$ lb. dried bilberries, $\frac{1}{2}$ lb. sultanas, $\frac{1}{2}$ 5 ml. spoonful citric acid, all-purpose wine yeast, nutrient, $\frac{1}{2}$ teaspoonful Pectinol, sugar: for dry 2 lb., for medium 2 lb. 10 oz., for sweet 3 lb., water as in method on page 92.

Rhubarb Wine (Another light claret style)

$1\frac{1}{2}$ lb. rhubarb, $\frac{1}{2}$ lb. dried currants, $\frac{1}{2}$ lb. dried elderberries, $\frac{1}{2}$ 5 ml. spoonful citric acid, all-purpose wine yeast, nutrient, $\frac{1}{2}$ level teaspoonful Pectinol, sugar: for dry 2 lb., for medium 2 lb. 12 oz., for sweet 3 lb., water as in method on page 92.

Rhubarb Wine (Rosé style)

2 lb. rhubarb, $1\frac{1}{2}$ lb. blackcurrants (or large bottle of Ribena), $\frac{1}{2}$ lb. sultanas, all-purpose wine yeast, nutrient, $\frac{1}{2}$ level teaspoonful Pectinol, sugar: for dry 2 lb., for medium $2\frac{3}{4}$ lb., for sweet 3 lb., water as in method on page 92.

Rhubarb Wine (Another Rosé style)

2 lb. rhubarb, $\frac{1}{2}$ lb. dried sloes, 1 lb. raisins, all-purpose wine yeast, nutrient, $\frac{1}{2}$ level teaspoonful Pectinol, sugar: for dry $1\frac{3}{4}$ lb., for medium $2\frac{1}{4}$ lb., for sweet $2\frac{1}{2}$ lb., water as in method on page 92.

Rhubarb Wine (Another Rosé)

2 lb. rhubarb, 2×15 oz. tins of loganberries (or the equivalent), $\frac{1}{2}$ lb. sultanas, all-purpose wine yeast, nutrient, $\frac{1}{2}$ level teaspoonful Pectinol, sugar: for dry 2 lb., for medium 2 lb 10 oz., for sweet 3 lb., water as in method on page 92.

Rhubarb and Dried Prune (Could be called a claret-Rosé)

2 lb. rhubarb, $\frac{3}{4}$ lb. dried prunes, (or 2 lb. tinned prunes in syrup), $\frac{1}{2}$ 5 ml. spoonful citric acid, all-purpose wine yeast, nutrient, $\frac{1}{2}$ level teaspoonful Pectinol, sugar: for dry 2 lb., for medium $2\frac{1}{2}$ lb., for sweet $2\frac{3}{4}$ lb., water as in method on page 92.

Method for Rhubarb Wine

Before you begin, dried bilberries and sloes must be washed under a fast running tap. Rhubarb should be weighed after the leaves and stumps have been cut off and the sticks wiped clean with a damp cloth. Pre-packed raisins and sultanas need not be washed, but these should be chopped or minced finely before they are put into the fermenting vessel. Prunes should be stoned and cut up small.

Cut the rhubarb into small lengths and crush with a rolling pin, being careful not to lose any juice. Put these in the fermenting pail with the other fruits or juices required. Add the acid where called for and pour on about half a gallon of boiling water. Put the sugar in a saucepan with about a quart of water, bring slowly to the boil stirring frequently and then pour this into the mixture. The next step is to make up the mixture to about five quarts with boiling water. Allow to cool to lukewarm. Then crush one Campden fruit preserving tablet to a powder and dissolve this in about half a cupful of warm water. Stir this into the mixture and then give the lot a thorough churning. Having done this add the yeast and nutrient. Cover as advised and put the mixture in the warm to ferment for seven or eight days, stirring daily. After this strain out the pulp through three or four thicknesses of muslin and wring out as dry as you can. Clean the fermenting vessel and return the strained wine to this. Cover again as before and keep the mixture in the warm to continue fermenting for a further three or four days.

Having done this pour the wine carefully into a gallon jar leaving as much deposit in the pail as you can. Stir the Pectinol into the wine and if the jar is not filled to where the neck begins, fill to this level with boiled cooled water, then fit a fermentation lock and leave until all fermentation has ceased.

Thirteen

Making Wines from Vegetables

For years I had been thinking that the interest in making wines from vegetables was on the wane. Needless to say I am now surprised and delighted to find the interest as lively as ever, because I still make them myself – incorporating all sorts of ideas for new recipes. It seems that despite the popularity and convenience of pre-packed, tinned, dried and bottled ingredients which are ready to use, there is something special about wines made from vegetables, although one needs to spend a little more time preparing them. I am well aware that making top-class wines from certain vegetables offers a challenge and I have yet to meet the wine-maker who will not rise to meet it.

There is no doubt that wines made from vegetables are in a class of their own. Indeed, many a true countryman swears that there is no wine, commercial or home-made, that can compare with his two-year-old parsnip. And you'd better duck quickly if you contradict him! Many years ago, long before I decided to write about making wines, I evolved a recipe for using potatoes, raisins, oranges and a few other odds and ends and it became world famous. In this country alone over a hundred thousand readers of the *Daily Mirror* were using it, even before my first book was published. That recipe is now the property of many others.

One snag with making wines from certain vegetables is that a clearing problem often arises owing to pectin as well as starch being boiled into the must in the early stages. This is quite often avoided if the yeast is starved of sugar during the early stages of production. This induces the yeast to convert the starch to sugar and to ferment it – thus leaving a brilliant wine. But like all good plans, often this one comes unstuck. We then have to resort to using a starch-destroying enzyme – which is a very simple matter. And I prefer to see if the wine will clear itself rather than use a clarifier. I wait to see whether the wine is nearly brilliant as fermentation ceases and I then know from my long experience whether the wine will clear to brilliance or not. If I decide that it will not, I mix in a little Fungal Amylase – which is a starch-destroying enzyme. More about this later.

Since many vegetables contain pectin which we know causes cloudiness in fruit wines if not treated, it is wise to use Pectinol in these wines in the same way as in fruit wines.

An interesting test can be carried out with wines or musts prepared from vegetables to find out whether they contain starch or pectin or both. To test for pectin take one fluid ounce of the wine or must and add three or four ounces of methylated spirits. If Pectin is present, jelly-like clots or strings will form according to the extent of pectin present. The sample must be discarded. To test wines or a prepared must for the presence of starch take a small sample and add a few drops of tincture of iodine. If the sample turns blue, starch is present. To check this test for your own interest, slice a small potato in half and let a drop of iodine fall on to the freshly cut surface and watch it turn blue. Another important point is that all roots must be boiled for fifteen minutes to destroy soil bacteria.

Parsnip Wines (1)

4 lb. parsnips, 1 lb. sultanas, 2 level 5 ml. spoonfuls citric acid, 2 oranges, all-purpose wine yeast, nutrient, $\frac{1}{2}$ level teaspoonful Pectinol, $\frac{1}{2}$ pt. strong tea, sugar: for dry $1\frac{1}{2}$ lb., for medium $2\frac{1}{4}$., for sweet $2\frac{1}{2}$ lb., water as in method on page 95.

Parsnip Wines (2)

4 lb. parsnips, $\frac{3}{4}$ pt. Hock type concentrate, $1\frac{1}{2}$ level 5 ml. spoonfuls citric acid, all-purpose wine yeast, $\frac{1}{2}$ level teaspoon-

ful Pectinol, $\frac{1}{2}$ pt. strong tea, sugar: for dry 1$\frac{3}{4}$ lb., for medium 2$\frac{3}{4}$ lb., for sweet 2$\frac{1}{2}$ lb., water as in method below.

Carrot Wines (1)

4 lb. carrots, 1 lb. sultanas, 2 level 5 ml. spoonfuls citric acid, 3 oranges, all-purpose wine yeast, nutrient, $\frac{1}{2}$ level teaspoonful Pectinol, $\frac{1}{2}$ pt. strong tea, sugar: for dry 1$\frac{1}{2}$ lb., for medium 2$\frac{1}{4}$ lb., for sweet 2$\frac{1}{2}$ lb., water as in method below.

Carrot Wines (2)

4 lb. carrots, $\frac{1}{2}$ pt. Rosé concentrate, 1$\frac{1}{2}$ level 5 ml. spoonfuls citric acid, all-purpose wine yeast, nutrient, $\frac{1}{2}$ level teaspoonful Pectinol, $\frac{1}{2}$ pt. strong tea, sugar: for dry 2 lb., for medium 2$\frac{1}{2}$ lb., for sweet 2$\frac{3}{4}$ lb., water as in method below.

Method for Parsnip and Carrot Wines

Scrub the carrots or parsnips thoroughly, cutting out any eyes containing dirt and remove any blemishes. Then grate the roots, put them in about half a gallon of water, bring them to the boil and simmer gently for fifteen minutes taking off all scum that rises. Put half the sugar in the fermenting pail with the chopped sultanas (where these are being used) and strain the boiling roots through three or four thicknesses of muslin on to them (if using grape juice wait till mixture is cool). Add the citric acid and tea and stir until the sugar is dissolved. Then make up to about five quarts with boiling water. Allow the mixture to cool and then stir in the strained juice of the oranges where being used, and add the concentrated grape juice. Add the yeast and nutrient, cover the vessel as advised and leave the mixture in the warm to ferment for eight or nine days, stirring daily.

Having done this, strain out any solids present through

three or four thicknesses of muslin, wring out as dry as you can, clean the fermenting vessel and return the strained wine to this. Put the remaining sugar in about a pint of water (not more) and bring it slowly to the boil stirring frequently. Allow to cool a little and then stir this into the wine. Cover again as before and leave in the warm to ferment for a further three or four days. Then pour carefully into a warmed gallon jar, leaving as much deposit in the pail as you can. Stir in the Pectinol and if the jar is not filled to where the neck begins, fill to this level with boiled cooled water. Then fit a fermentation lock and leave until all fermentation has ceased.

Pea Pod Wines (1)

3½ lb. pea pods (peas must not be allowed into the mixture), 1 lb. sultanas, 3 oranges, 1½ level 5 ml. spoonfuls citric acid, all-purpose wine yeast, nutrient, ½ level teaspoonful Pectinol, ½ pt. strong tea, sugar: for dry 1¾ lb., for medium 2¼ lb., for sweet 2½ lb., water as in method on page 97.

Pea Pod Wines (2)

3½ lb. pea pods (peas must not be allowed into the mixture), ¾ pt. Hock type concentrate, 1 level 5 ml. spoonful citric acid, all-purpose wine yeast, nutrient, ½ level teaspoonful Pectinol, ½ pt. strong tea, sugar: for dry 1¾ lb., for medium 2¼ lb., for sweet 2½ lb., water as in method on page 97.

Parsley Wines (1)

1½ lb. young fresh parsley, ¾ lb. sultanas, 3 oranges, 1½ level 5 ml. spoonfuls citric acid, all-purpose wine yeast, nutrient, ½ level teaspoonful Pectinol, ½ pt. strong tea, sugar: for dry 2 lb., for medium 2 lb. 6 oz., for sweet 2 lb. 10 oz., water as in method on page 97.

Parsley Wines (2)

$1\frac{1}{2}$ lb. young fresh parsley, $\frac{1}{2}$ pt. Hock type concentrate, $1\frac{1}{2}$ level 5 ml. spoonfuls citric acid, all-purpose wine yeast, nutrient, $\frac{1}{2}$ level teaspoonful Pectinol, $\frac{1}{2}$ pt. strong tea, sugar: for dry 2 lb., for medium $2\frac{1}{2}$ lb., for sweet $2\frac{3}{4}$ lb., water as in method below.

Note: If fresh parsley is not available you may use 3 oz. of dried parsley, bearing in mind that 2 oz. represents the approximate equivalent of one pound of fresh parsley.

Method for Pea Pod and Parsley Wines

The fact that there are two recipes for pea pod wine and two for parsley wine does not mean that one is better than the other – but different they certainly are.

No. 1 Pea Pod wine is more of a social wine. In other words, it is more suitable for taking at any time, particularly in the evening when there is not necessarily food being eaten with it. No. 2 may be used in the same way, but if you wish to choose the one most suitable for use with food then No. 2 is the better. Exactly the same applies to parsley wine Nos 1 and 2. However, as with the whole of this business, personal preference is what counts most, so you will most likely ignore what I have said and do exactly the reverse – or both.

Thoroughly wash the pods or parsley (do not wash dried parsley), put them in enough water to cover well, bring to the boil and simmer for twenty minutes with the lid on. Put half the sugar in the fermenting pail with the chopped sultanas if being used (do not add grape juice at this stage). Strain the pod or parsley water through three or four thicknesses of muslin on to the sugar and sultanas and press out all the juice. Stir until the sugar is dissolved, then make up to about seven pints with boiling water. Grate the orange peel (where oranges are being used) into the mixture, then halve them, squeeze out the juice, strain it and add it to the rest. Having done this add the acid and tea. Allow the mixture to cool well, then stir in the grape juice (if being used) and then add the yeast and nutrient. Cover as advised and keep in the warm to ferment for seven or eight days, stirring daily. The next step is to strain out the solids through three or four thicknesses of muslin and wring out as dry as you can. Clean the fermenting vessel and return the strained wine to this. Boil remaining sugar in about a pint of water, stirring constantly. Allow this to cool and stir it into the wine. Cover again as before and leave in the warm for a further three or four days. Then pour carefully into a gallon jar, leaving as much deposit in the pail as you can. Stir in the Pectinol and if the jar is not filled to where the neck begins, fill to this level with boiled cooled water, then fit a fermentation lock and leave until all fermentation has ceased.

Note: In the above method, where no solids are present as when grape juice is being used, there will be no need to strain the wine after seven or eight days. Merely boil the sugar at this stage, as advised, and add it to the wine, then leave in the vessel for the stipulated three or four days.

Potato Wines (1)

2 lb. old potatoes, 1½ lb. raisins, 3 oranges, 1½ level 5 ml. spoonfuls citric acid, all-purpose wine yeast, nutrient, ½ level teaspoonful Pectinol, ½ pt. strong tea, sugar: (do *not* make a dry potato wine), for medium 2 lb., for sweet 2¼ lb., water as in method on page 99.

Potato Wines (2)

2 lb. old potatoes, ¾ pt. Hock type concentrate, 3 oranges, 1½ level 5 ml. spoonfuls citric acid, ½ level teaspoonful Pectinol, ½ pt. strong tea, sugar: (do *not* make a dry potato wine), for medium 2 lb., for sweet 2¼ lb., water as in method on page 99.

Mangold Wine (1) (Mangel-Wurzel) An old country favourite

4 lb. mangolds, 1½ lb. raisins, 3 oranges, 1½ level 5 ml. spoon-

fuls citric acid, all-purpose wine yeast, nutrient, $\frac{1}{2}$ level teaspoonful Pectinol, $\frac{1}{2}$ pt. strong tea, sugar: for dry $1\frac{1}{2}$ lb., for
medium 2 lb., for sweet $2\frac{1}{4}$ lb., water as in method below.

Mangold Wines (2)

4 lb. mangolds, $\frac{1}{2}$ pt. Rosé concentrate, 3 oranges, $1\frac{1}{2}$ level
5 ml. spoonfuls citric acid, $\frac{1}{2}$ level teaspoonful Pectinol, $\frac{1}{2}$ pt.
strong tea, sugar: for dry 2 lb., for medium $2\frac{1}{2}$ lb., for sweet
$2\frac{3}{4}$ lb., water as in method below.

Method for Potato and Mangold Wines

Scrub the potatoes or mangolds without peeling them.
Remove any eyes or crevices containing dirt and remove any
blemishes. Cut them up or grate them. Mangolds are sometimes a bit stringy in the middle end and if this is so cut this up
rather than try to grate it. Put the prepared roots in about
half a gallon of water, bring slowly to the boil and simmer
for fifteen minutes, taking off any scum that rises. Put roughly
half the sugar in the fermenting pail with the chopped raisins
and strain the boiling root water through three or four thicknesses of muslin on to them. Gather up the straining cloths
and press out the water – a bread board and kitchen cutting
board from either side will prevent scalded fingers.

Having done this stir thoroughly to dissolve the sugar, next
add the citric acid and tea and make up to about five quarts
with boiling water. Allow the mixture to cool well, and where
oranges are being used, grate the peel into the mixture, cut the
oranges in half, press out the juice, strain it and add this to
the rest. Add the concentrated grape juice if being used. Then
add the yeast and nutrient. Cover as advised and keep in the
warm to ferment for seven or eight days, stirring daily. Having
done this, strain out any solids present through three or four
thicknesses of muslin, wring out as dry as you can, clean the
fermenting vessel and return the strained wine to this. Put the
remaining sugar in not more than a pint of water, bring it
slowly to the boil stirring frequently. Allow this to cool a

little and then stir it into the wine. Cover as before and leave
in the warm to ferment for a further three or four days. Then
pour carefully into a previously warmed gallon jar, leaving
as much deposit in the pail as you can. Stir in the Pectinol
and if the jar is not filled to where the neck begins, fill to this
level with boiled cooled water, then fit a fermentation lock
and leave until all fermentation has ceased.

Note: In the above method, where there are no solids present
as when grape concentrate is being used, there will be no need
to strain the wine. Therefore, when straining would normally
be carried out after seven or eight days, merely boil the sugar
as advised, let this cool well and then stir it into the wine and
leave for the extra three or four days.

Using Fungal Amylase

It will be seen in the recipes that I recommend the use of
Pectinol. The idea here is to destroy any pectin present in the
vegetables. Most contain a small amount of this and it will do
no harm to use the Pectinol even if the pectin content of the
vegetable is practically nil. Similarly, the amount of starch in
vegetables varies enormously and whether a starch-destroying
enzyme is necessary to clear the wine depends on how well
the plan to starve the yeast of sugar and so induce it to
convert the starch to sugar and ferment it works out. I have
mentioned this at the beginning of this chapter. If your
vegetable wines do not clear as fermentation nears completion
it would be wise to use a little Fungal Amylase to destroy the
starch which is holding minute solids in suspension causing
the cloudiness. The amount suggested by the manufacturers
is 2.5 grams to five gallons. If treating one gallon spread a
capful from the container on to a piece of clean paper and
divide roughly into quarters and then mix a quarter with a
little of the wine and then stir it into the bulk. This will be a
little more than is needed but it will do no harm. If you
happen to be racking the wine when the Fungal Amylase is to
be added, mix it with a little of the wine, put it in the empty
jar and fill up with the wine.

Fourteen

Making Wines from Apples

It is always best to use a mixture of apples to obtain the best results. It is often wise too, to use apples as a basic ingredient in the same way as I have suggested for rhubarb. If you happen to grow apples you have the basics of some really delightful wines, for all you need is a pound or so of some popular dried or fresh fruit such as elderberries, sloes, damsons or blackberries. Even a bottle of Ribena or some other similar blackcurrant syrup added to a gallon of wine being made from say eight pounds of apples will make a wine quite out of the ordinary. These recipes will be especially useful to those who grow apples in this country, in Canada and the USA where thousands of tons are thrown away each year.

Apples contain pectin and a little starch so it may be necessary in the later stages of production to use a little Fungal Amylase as has been discussed in the section on clarifying wines.

Each wine will vary slightly depending on the variety of apples used, though it does not matter which sort you choose, except that it is always wise to use two or three varieties and incorporate twenty-five per cent of the cooking variety.

The following recipe (one for three types of wines) is a basic recipe which will make a pleasant wine in its own right. Immediately following the method is a list of other ingredients that may be added without altering the basic recipe at all. Working in this way we find that there are very many wines that can be made from the basic materials, recipe and method.

Apple Wines

8 lb. apples (10 lb. if making sweet wine), 1 lb. sultanas, all-

purpose wine yeast, nutrient, $\frac{1}{2}$ level teaspoonful Pectinol, sugar: for dry $1\frac{3}{4}$ lb., for medium $2\frac{1}{4}$ lb., for sweet $2\frac{1}{2}$ lb., water as in method below.

The following is a list of ingredients and the most suitable quantities that may be added to the apple wine recipe without altering any of the basic ingredients. If you add any of these, add them at the same time as adding the sultanas. If using the dried fruits mentioned, wash them thoroughly before adding.

Elderberries	2 lb. fresh	or $\frac{1}{2}$ lb. dried.
Sloes	1 lb. ,,	or $\frac{1}{4}$ lb. ,,
Bilberries	2 lb. ,,	or $\frac{1}{2}$ lb. ,,
Blackberries	$2\frac{1}{2}$ lb. ,,	or equivalent tinned
Loganberries	2 lb. ,,	or ,,
Damsons	2 lb. ,,	or ,,
Plums (red)	$2\frac{1}{2}$ lb. ,,	or ,,
Blackcurrants	2 lb. ,,	or about $1\frac{1}{2}$ pts. black-currant syrup – not cordial.
Prunes	nil	approx. 2 lb. tinned

Note: 'Equivalent tinned' above. You need not be exact here. A few ounces short will not matter all that much, and it might not be possible to obtain the exact weight when buying tinned ingredients.

Method for Apple Wines

Crush one and a half Campden fruit preserving tablets into a powder and dissolve this in a little warm water. Put half a gallon of boiled cooled water into the fermenting pail and stir in the Campden solution. Thoroughly wash the apples, cut out any blemishes but do not peel them. Then core them and put them through the coarse plate of the mincer, one at a time, and put the minced pulp into the pail at once – this is to prevent browning. Instead of mincing, you can use the pulper of a fruit juice extractor if you have one. Either way be careful not to lose any juice. Having done this add the chopped sultanas and make up the mixture to one gallon with water.

Put half the sugar in a saucepan with a quart of water, bring slowly to the boil stirring frequently. When boiling, stir into the mixture. Then add the Pectinol. Cover as advised and leave for twenty-four hours in a warm place, stirring occasionally.

The next step is to give the mixture a thorough stirring and add the yeast and nutrient. Cover again as before and keep the must in the warm to ferment for six or seven days, stirring daily. After this, strain through three or four thicknesses of muslin and wring out as dry as you can. Clean the fermenting vessel and return the strained wine to this. Put the remaining sugar in the saucepan with one pint of water, bring it slowly to the boil stirring frequently, allow it to cool and then stir it into the wine. Cover as before and leave in the warm to ferment for a further five or six days – or a day or two longer if fermentation is still vigorous.

The next step is to pour carefully into a gallon jar leaving as much deposit behind as you can. If the jar is not filled to where the neck begins, fill to this level with boiled cooled water, then fit a fermentation lock and leave in the warm until all fermentation has ceased.

Fifteen

Making Wines from Flowers

Flower wines will always be popular – especially amongst those living within easy reach of the flowers of the country-side. The delicately aromatic flavours of wines made from flowers has to be savoured to be believed. But it is not just the flavours of these wines that makes them so popular, it is the aroma and bouquet that comes with them. Those who want to make flower wines may use dried flowers – though the best results are obtained from those fresh from the countryside or – if you grow roses – from the garden.

I used to use what is known as synthetic must in flower wines because this acted as a basic fermentable medium which is necessary if good results are to be obtained when making wines from flowers. The fact is that the flowers alone with just sugar and yeast and some acid and tannin added would not form a suitable must either from the fermentability of it or from the point of view of producing quality wines. We must look to other ingredients to form the basis of a ferment-able must and therefore quality wine, and we can choose either concentrated grape juice or sultanas. If used in the quantities recommended the flavour given into the wines by these ingredients will not be sufficient to alter or lessen the the flavour given into them by the flowers – which is, of course, what we want.

It will be seen in the recipes that I recommend sultanas with varying amounts of sugar for the differing wine types – dry, sweet, etc. Under each recipe appears the name of a grape juice, the quantity to use and varied amounts of sugar. If you use the basic recipe and do not want to use grape juice, ignore this. But if you decide to try grape juice, use this with the varying amounts of sugar and leave out the sultanas and the amounts of sugar recommended for use with them in the basic recipe.

Bananas may be used with flower wines in addition to other ingredients suggested. A note at the end of this chapter explains what to do.

When gathering flowers avoid picking them by main roads, otherwise you may find them contaminated with exhaust fumes. Only the heads of dandelions should be taken and these should be pinched off to avoid taking even the tiniest part of the stem which contains a bitter 'milk'; if the stem is taken this might contaminate the petals. Dandelions close up after being gathered, and to remove the petals, hold the green calix in one hand and with the other, pull off all the petals in one go.

Although I do not regard flowers as being suitable for sweet wines, I include the amount of sugar to produce a sweet wine if you want to try this.

When measuring flowers – petals only – put them in a pint or quart jug. Do not press them down by hand, but merely bump the jug on a suitable surface to settle them and then fill up the jug.

It will be seen that the recipes are followed by one method on page 106 which is suitable for all the recipes.

Rose Petal Wines (Use scented roses)

4 to 5 pints rose petals, 1 lb. sultanas, $1\frac{1}{2}$ level 5 ml. spoonfuls citric acid, $\frac{1}{2}$ pt. strong tea, all-purpose wine yeast, nutrient, sugar: for dry 2 lb., for medium $2\frac{1}{4}$ lb., for sweet $2\frac{1}{2}$ lb., water as in method on page 106.

If you want to use grape concentrate instead of sultanas, use $\frac{1}{2}$ pt. Rosé. The above amounts of sugar will be satisfactory.

Dandelion Wines

3 quarts petals, 1 lb. sultanas, $\frac{1}{2}$ pt. strong tea, 2 level 5 ml. spoonfuls citric acid, all-purpose wine yeast, nutrient, sugar:

for dry 2 lb., for medium 2¼ lb., for sweet 2½ lb., water as in method below.

If you want to use grape concentrate instead of sultanas, use ¾ pt. Hock type and reduce the above amounts of sugar by 2 oz. in each case.

Elderflower Wines

When gathering the florets you may notice trees with almost perfectly rounded flower heads about the size of a saucer. Use these, not those from other trees with larger heads of rather irregular shape. Fewer flowers are needed for elderflower wines owing to their pungence.

1 to 1½ pt. elderflowers, 1 lb. sultanas, ½ pt. strong tea, 1½ level 5 ml. spoonfuls citric acid, all-purpose wine yeast, nutrient, sugar: for dry 2 lb., for medium 2¼ lb., for sweet 2½ lb., water as in method below.

If you want to use grape concentrate instead of sultanas, use ½ pt. Hock type. The above amounts of sugar will be satisfactory.

Hawthorn Flower Wines (May Blossom)

2 pt. hawthorn blossom, 1 lb. sultanas, ½ pt. strong tea, 1½ level 5 ml. spoonfuls citric acid, all-purpose wine yeast, nutrient, sugar: for dry 2 lb., for medium 2¼ lb., for sweet 2½ lb., water as in method below.

If you want to use grape concentrate instead of sultanas, use ½ pt. Hock type with the amounts of sugar given in the basic recipe.

Method for Flower Wines

Put the chopped sultanas or grape juice in the fermenting pail. Put the sugar in about a quart of water, bring it to the boil slowly, stirring frequently and when cooled well, stir

into the pail. Stir in the strained tea and acid and make up
the mixture to one gallon. Crush and dissolve one Campden
tablet to a powder, dissolve this in a little warm water and stir
into the bulk. Then give a thorough stirring and stir in the
flowers. Having done this add the yeast and nutrient. Cover as
advised and leave to ferment for five or six days stirring
daily. The next step is to strain the wine through three or
or four thicknesses of muslin and to wring out fairly dry.
Clean the fermenting vessel and return the strained wine to
this. Cover as before and leave in the warm to ferment for a
further five or six days, then pour carefully into a gallon jar
leaving as much deposit behind as you can. If the jar is not
filled to where the neck begins, fill to this level with boiled
cooled water, then fit a fermentation lock and leave until all
fermentation has ceased.

Using Bananas in Flower Wines

The first thing to bear in mind when contemplating using
bananas where they are not included in the recipe is that one
pound of bananas without their skins contains roughly five
ounces of sugar. This would have to be taken into account.
The skinned bananas must be mashed to pulp with a fork and
then put into enough water to cover them well. After this they
should be brought to the boil slowly and simmered for twenty
minutes. Do use a saucepan twice the size you would normally
use because bananas rise up a great deal on boiling. Allow
the boiled material to cool and then stir it into the must if
you are fermenting a pulp (ingredients) for not more than
five days. If you are to ferment for more than five days as in
the above method it would be best to strain out the fluffy
banana residue and to add only the liquid.

Sixteen

Making Meads

As I have written elsewhere, mead is one of the oldest known alcoholic drinks. It is believed to have come about more or less by accident, which could be said of all wines for that matter. After all, the yeast to make the wine is already on the fruits and even if this is contaminated by undesirable yeast, a wine of sorts would result when the fruits fall to the ground, are gathered up and allowed to rot. Indeed, I have seen pigs as drunk as lords after eating through a mound of rotting apples that must have been fermenting for some time. But the meads made by accident and those made today are, naturally, vastly different. Indeed, many swear that there is not a wine that can compare with honey wine. I have made many types of mead from different honies, and what follows is the secret of making the mead most likely to suit you.

Many people are satisfied with mead made from blended honies, but to obtain a really first class product one type of honey only should be used. It is a fact that many people taking holidays in Devon, Cornwall and other areas where mead is made in large quantities by many people, often ask me how to make mead like they make in . . . , or wherever they have been. The first thing I ask is if they know which honey was used. They never know, probably because they never thought to ask. For this reason they may never make mead quite like the one they have tasted. There are many kinds of honies, all peculiar to the areas in which they are made, and these are the best to use – especially those known as comb honies. These are pure honies whilst most others are blended, containing several different kinds of pure honey and perhaps some invert sugar. It is best, therefore, to obtain your honey from an apiarist (bee-keeper) in your area – if you can. Otherwise you may buy bulk lots of blended honey from home wine supply firms. If you buy the small half pound jars to make mead it will cost you a fortune. One seven pound tin from a supply firm will enable you to make one gallon of sweet and one gallon of dry mead. Bear in mind that honey is approximately 75 per cent sugar.

As with all wine-making, a good fermentation is essential. Because honey does not contain acid or tannin we must add both – sugar is, of course, not needed. A good general purpose wine yeast together with a good nutrient should combine to make an excellent product.

Four pounds of honey will make a sweet mead while three pounds will make a dry one. Remember that what is sweet to some people is over-sweet to others. Similarly, what is dry to some is much too dry for others. Therefore, there will be some sort of trial and error in this respect before you can make precisely the mead you are aiming at. Using the hydrometer as explained on pp. 38-43 will also be helpful.

The first step is to decide whether you want a dry, medium or sweet mead, and then work in the following manner, bearing in mind that 3 lb. of honey will make a dry mead, $3\frac{1}{2}$ lb. will make a medium, and 4 lb. will make a sweet mead.

You will also need for one gallon, half a pint of freshly-made strong tea, one heaped teaspoonful of acid blend or $1\frac{1}{2}$ level 5 ml. spoonfuls of citric acid.

Method

Mix the honey with about half a gallon of hot water, bring to the boil stirring frequently and then boil for two minutes. Pour into the fermenting pail, add the citric acid and tea and make up to one gallon with boiling water, or boiled water that has cooled. Allow the mixture to cool, then add the yeast and nutrient. Thereafter proceed as for all other wines.

Flavoured meads

There are many ways in which you can produce a wide variety of flavoured meads using flowers – clover, gorse flowers, rose petals and so on. The amounts to use are really a matter of choice depending on the strength of flavour required, remembering that the flavour of the honey should always be allowed to predominate. The amounts I have used in various trials with good results are:

Rose petals (scented), 2 pints
Gorse flowers, 2 pints
Clover (mauve only), 2 pints
Dandelions (petals only), 3 pints
Elderflowers, $\frac{1}{2}$ pint
Hawthorn blossom (May blossom), 1 pint
Lime flowers, 2 pints

If you use flowers, add them to the fermenting pail and pour on the boiling honey mixture. Ferment for seven days, then strain out the flowers, return the strained mead to the fermenting pail. Continue to ferment for three or four more days, then pour into a gallon jar, leaving as much deposit behind as you can. If the jar is not filled to where the neck begins, fill to this level with boiled water that has cooled. Then fit a fermentation lock and leave until all fermentation has ceased.

Part Two

Home
Beer-Making

Seventeen

The Beginner's Guide to Beer-Making

Like wine-making, beer-making is booming as never before. Indeed, it has become so popular that giants like Reckitt and Colman, the mustard people, as well as many others, have jumped on to the wagon of the supply trade with kits from which all kinds of beers are made for about three pence a pint. The kits are available, with full instructions, at most wine supply firms (see list at the end of this book) as well as at health food stores and the larger multiple chemists.

But do not imagine that the first attempt will make your favourite mild and bitter as you buy it down at the local, or your Guinness and mild, or light and bitter or whichever your bad habit is. What's wrong with a bad habit or two – you don't get much fun out of the good ones!

These beer kits produce beers which are, like most wine recipes, designed to meet the demands of the average palate. As there is really no such thing as the average palate any more than there is a typical Irishman, American, or any other national for that matter, it all boils down to the manufacturers producing a wort (this is the equivalent to a must in wine-making) which will turn out a beer that will be as near as possible to the liking of as many people as possible and one that will be easy to acquire a taste for.

I have come across some blokes who did not like their first beer, but its cheapness was not to be sniffed at – nor were their first two or three tries! But later they began to like it – in other words, they had acquired the taste for it. Others, more fastidious and discerning, decided that once they had mastered the technique of using the ready-made worts in

113

cans, turned to blending their own ingredients – various types of malts, hops, etc., to make a beer that they really wanted. And there is the secret of successful beer-making. Obtain your experience with easy-to-use materials and then graduate to using the raw materials to produce the very kind of beer you have been looking for. This involves choosing between the various malts and malt extracts and hops.

Later, if you want to you can use grain malts. The difference is that malt extracts, whether they are in syrup form or dried, are malts extracted from the grain whereas malts are, strictly speaking, malts still within the grain. The difference in the flavours of the various extracts and grain malts depends upon the processes they have been put through, toasting, roasting, etc., and the fact is that you can learn to make beers better than those bought over the bar. This is not difficult to understand, because nowadays brewers are using less malt, which gives flavour and body to your beer and using more sugar which gives precious little to the beer except the amount of alcohol the yeast can make from it. When less sugar and more malt is used the fermentable sugars present in the malt are used up by the yeast, but the flavours are left in the beers though, like the flavours of fruits in wine-making, these flavours are changed so that you obtain flavours produced from malt rather than the flavour of the malt itself – though some of it may still linger.

When using the prepared worts – that is those in cans – it is of the utmost importance to follow the directions of the supplier, for the very simple reason that he has formulated the wort and therefore knows the method best suited to making the kind of beer the wort is designed for.

When you set out on your own with malt extracts, you start making beers halfway through the process. This is because you are not putting grain malts through what is known as the mashing period. The mashing period is the time when the malted barley is cracked and steeped in water (brewery liquor) in the mash tun, and kept at varying temperatures so that enzymes bring about desirable changes. When the changes have taken place the wort is poured off the near spent grain into coppers where it is boiled with hops. Boiling 'fixes' the beer. In other words, boiling halts all enzyme action because it destroys them. Boiling is also necessary in order to destroy any wild yeasts and bacteria that may be present and therefore capable of spoiling your beer in the same way as they spoil wines. The wort is then cooled to about 60° F. and the yeast 'pitched' in (added). It is wise to have this ready as a nucleus as in wine-making. Shortly after the yeast is pitched in the transformation into beer begins.

When using malt extracts, this mashing period is not necessary because the malts that would be extracted during mashing are already in your hands either in the form of syrup or as a powder. So using malt extracts is the next simplest form of beer making to using the ready prepared worts in cans, and should come as second nature to anybody who has used them.

Utensils

It is best to obtain utensils from home-brew supply outlets; you are then assured that they are made of suitable materials. A five-gallon fermenting vessel is ideal for a four-gallon brew because it allows for expansion during fermentation and the nobbly yeast head that forms. You will need a Burco or similar type of boiler to hold three gallons. This allows for two gallons

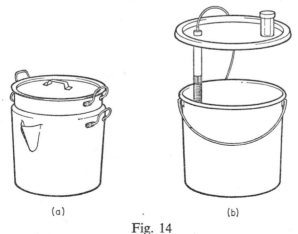

(a)   (b)

Fig. 14

or a little more to be boiled and allows for headroom. This
is satisfactory for a four-gallon brew because the wort can be
made up to four gallons with boiling water at a later stage.
Naturally, if you make two-gallon lots a three-gallon size
fermentation vessel will be large enough. A deep, very fine
mesh sieve is an asset though many brewers manage with
three or four thicknesses of muslin. An important item is a
thermometer of the sort used in jam-making. This will be used
to check the temperature of your worts. You will also need a
funnel at least nine inches in diameter at the top.

Bottling

Bottling the finished beer is a big job, but this is no longer
quite so necessary unless you insist upon bottled beer quality
in all your brews.The beer can be fermented out – sweetened
if necessary as explained later – and put into the latest item to
come on to the market. This is a plastic barrel with a CO_2
gas cylinder attached with a valve to enable you to charge

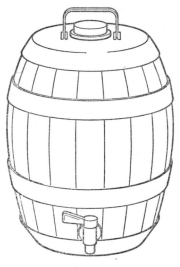

Fig. 15

the barrel with gas to prevent the beer going flat or losing its quality. If put into a barrel or a stone jar with a tap only the air drawn in as the beer is run off is above the beer. This can cause trouble if the beer is not used up quickly. The barrel with its gas cylinder works on the same principle as its smaller counterpart, the Sparklet siphon, with which some people contrive to make their wines semi-sparkling.

But this sort of thing can wait until you are a little more experienced.

If bottling beers you will need pint bottles, a crown corker, crown caps, and a hammer to clout the crown corker so that it presses the crown cap on to the bottle. A firm, sharp tap is all that is needed.

Water

Your ordinary water supply is quite suitable for beer-making in the early stages of your venture. But it is a fact that the water in many areas needs softening, or, in some cases hardening, depending on where you live and the type of beers being made. It is well known that certain breweries' beers are famous mainly because of their water supply. But you cannot expect to become a 'professional' brewer in a couple of months and it needs a good deal of experience before you can decide whether to treat the water or not. As with all things, experience is what counts and you can only obtain this by making a variety of beers by a variety of methods while using a variety of materials. By these means you will soon find the sort of beers you want to make.

Ingredients

Do bear in mind that it is useless to go to an ordinary chemist for your brewing malts, as the sorts they sell are mostly no good for beer-making. It is therefore essential to obtain all ingredients from suppliers of home-brewing equipment and ingredients.

Crown cap
as fitted to
beer bottles

Fig. 16

The Hydrometer

This is used in beer-making mainly to find the original gravity
of the wort before the yeast is added, the idea being to prevent
you making too strong beers. An initial gravity of 1050 giving
a potential alcohol content of 6 per cent is usually enough for
most beer. Indeed, many are lower than this while, it is
conceded, some are higher. High-alcohol beers will only make
you drunk very quickly – and there is no point in that. If you
find that the gravity is too high when the yeast is to be added
it can be reduced to the level required by diluting with boiled

cooled water. On the other hand, if the gravity is too low it
may be increased by adding sugar, bearing in mind that $2\frac{1}{4}$ oz.
will raise the gravity of one gallon by five degrees ($4\frac{1}{2}$ oz. will
raise it by five degrees in two gallons and so on). If you decide
to add sugar, take a little of the wort into a china, polythene
or Pyrex jug and add the sugar required, stand the jug in
water over heat, warm the water gently, stirring the sugar all
the time. In a few minutes it will be dissolved and then it
may be stirred into the wort.

Do bear in mind that I can give you only the basic ground-
ing in home-brewing within these pages – a book twice this
size could be written on the subject.

Nevertheless, there is enough information here to get you
off the ground and enough recipes to enable you to make some
decent beers. It will be for you as you progress to alter recipes
to suit yourself. Beers vary greatly with each brewer and
district so that light ales, pale ales, bitters, brown ales, mild
ales, stouts, all have markedly different characteristics peculiar
to the part of the country in which you happen to live. Therefore it may take a little time before you can make the kind
of beer you are used to. But this aspect should not bother you
too greatly. I say this because too many people try to imitate
commercial wines and beers when they have in their hands
the materials to make quite unique products, though I suppose
it is natural that when you like a certain commercial wine or
beer you want to make it like that yourself. I suppose I am
just as 'guilty' of this as most other blokes, after all, I like a
pint or two – or three – of home-brew as near like light and
bitter as I can get it.

Brewing Vocabulary

Beginners may be puzzled by terms used here and in the price
lists of various firms, in advertising matter and in other books
they may have. The following will clarify matters.

Bottom Fermenting Yeast. This yeast settles to the bottom of
the fermenting vessel (used mainly on the continent).

Condition. The state of beer brought about by gas produced during the fermentation of the priming sugar.

Cracked (or Crushed) Barley. Barley that has been prepared for use.

Dextrins. Essential substances found in wort during mashing.

Diastase. An enzyme in grain barley which converts starch to fermentable sugars.

Finings. Isinglass or other clarifying media such as Irish moss.

Grist. Malted and crushed barley ready for the mashing vessel, also any other additive such as flaked maize.

Lactose. Unfermentable milk sugar used to sweeten dark beers as required.

Lees. Deposit or waste matter that settles to the bottom of containers.

Malt. Malted barley otherwise malt still within the grain.

Malt Extract. Malt extracted from the grain and obtainable in the form of syrup or powder.

Pitching. Adding the yeast.

Priming. Adding sugar to fully fermented out beer to bring about renewed fermentation in the bottle.

Sparge (Sparging). The action of pouring further hot water through the grains or hops after the wort has been poured off.

Top Fermenting Yeast. Yeast that rises to the top of fermenting vessel (the yeast used in Britain).

Wort. The mixture during all stages of production until it is bottled or put into CO_2 charged containers.

Sweetening Beers

If you sweeten beer with ordinary sugar it will only be fermented out thereby increasing the alcohol content, making the beer too strong. We therefore use Lactose which is a milk sugar. This is not fermentable by beer or wine yeasts. Two to three ounces is usually enough for one gallon but this will depend very much, like so many other aspects in brewing, upon personal tastes.

Do remember when altering recipes or formulating your own that more malt will add more flavour and body while more hops will add a little more tang or bitterness – more bite. It is always wise to try small amounts of differing malts or malt extracts while using pale malts or malt extracts as the basis for all beers.

When using grain malts obtain already cracked grains. I advise this because crushing or cracking the grains is quite a skilled job that can, if not carried out properly, result in a very poor extraction during mashing.

Maintaining Temperature

When making beers from grain malts a mashing period is necessary and it is of the utmost importance that the correct temperature be maintained – minus or plus one degree. If this is not done starches will not be converted, but will remain as starches to cloud or spoil the beer in other ways. Indeed, you may not obtain beer at all. If you have a gas cooker, the temperature can be maintained by moving the vessel over the pilot and wrapping it in a blanket to insulate it from the cool of the room. If you have an electric cooker this cannot be done so easily except where the controls can be regulated to a very fine degree. Some brewers use an immersion heater of the type used in tropical fish tanks with the thermostat set at the required level of temperature. When taking up brewing seriously – which of course is the best way to do it – it is wise to invest (and it *is* an investment) in a Burco boiler which has been specially designed for the purpose of brewing by amateurs. With this you can bring the water to the required temperature, stir in the malts, bring the wort back to the required temperature for the time required after which the wort can be boiled in the same container. This is available from Vinaide Brewing Products, 31 Blackfriars Road, Salford, Manchester 3. This boiler has many other uses besides that of brewing.

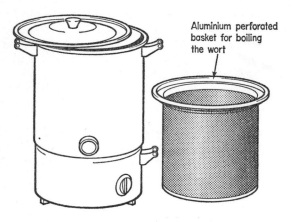

Aluminium perforated basket for boiling the wort

Fig. 17

Eighteen

Making Beer
with Malt
Extracts

The following recipes are for two-gallon lots. If you want to make four-gallon lots merely double the amounts of each ingredient listed.

Bitter

2 lb. pale malt extract, 4 oz. dried dark malt extract, 5 oz. crystal malt, $2\frac{1}{2}$ oz. hops, good beer yeast. Water as in method on page 124.

Mild Beer

2 lb. pale malt extract, 12 oz. dried medium dark or dark malt extract, $1\frac{1}{2}$ oz. hops, good beer yeast, water as in method on page 124.

Brown Ale

2 lb. pale malt extract, 12 oz. medium dark dried malt extract, 4 oz. crystal malt, 2 oz. hops, (Lactose to taste), water as in method on page 124.

Pale Ale (Light Ale)

$2\frac{1}{2}$ lb. pale malt extract, dried. 2 oz. hops, good beer yeast, water as in method on page 124.

Stout

1½ lb. pale malt extract, 12 oz. of both medium and dark dried malt extract, pinch salt, 1½ oz. hops, water as in method below.

Lager

3 bl. DMS malt extract, ½ lb. pale malt extract, 1¼ oz. hops. top fermenting lager yeast, ¼ level 5 ml. spoonful citric acid, pinch salt, water as in method below.

Strong Bitter

3 lb. pale malt extract, ½ lb. medium dark or dark dried malt extract, 1½ oz. hops, ¼ level 5 ml. spoonful citric acid, pinch salt, water as in method below. Raise gravity to 1055 maximum.

Porter Type

1½ lb. pale malt extract, 12 oz. dark malt extract, bottom fermenting yeast, 1½ oz. hops, ¼ level 5 ml. spoonful citric acid, pinch salt, water as in method below.

Method for Making Beer with Malt Extracts

'Adjust the gravity.' When you come to this direction use the hydrometer (as advised in the wine-making chapters) to find the specific gravity and then adjust this, either increasing it by dissolving white sugar in the wort (bearing in mind that 2¼ oz. will increase the gravity by 5° F in one gallon – 4½ oz. in two gallons) or lower the reading by adding boiled water. You may decide before you do this the amount of alcohol you require in the beer by consulting the hydrometer table on page 41. But do not increase to too high an alcohol content. An initial gravity of between 1040 and 1060 is plenty, depending of course on the type of beer you are making.

If your largest vessel is not sufficient to hold two gallons leaving plenty of head room, use as much water as possible so as to leave the vessel one-third empty. This will allow for boiling up. Put the hops in about three pints of water, stir them well, bring to the boil and boil quickly for forty-five minutes.

Put the malt extracts into the boiling vessel and stir in enough hot water to dissolve them and stir well until thoroughly dissolved. The vessel will now be about three-quarters full. Bring to the boil, and maintain for five minutes. Strain the hops, add the water to the wort, bring it back to the boil for ten minutes and then pour the wort into the fermenting vessel. Having done this, make up the wort to two gallons with boiled cooled water. In this way you will bring the temperature of the whole down to about 60° F. Check the temperature as it should not be below 55° F. Adjust the gravity according to the amount of alcohol you want and then stir in the yeast.

Put the lid on the fermenting vessel or cover it as advised for wine-making and stir the wort twice at eight-hour intervals. When a yeast head forms skim it off and discard it. Stir once more and allow the new yeast head to remain. Take a hydrometer reading after three days and until the wort has fermented out to about 1010, then transfer to jars as used in wine-making, skim and fit fermentation locks. Allow the beer to ferment until it stops – keeping it warm of course. Then siphon it into the fermenting vessel leaving the deposit behind. For two gallons dissolve $4\frac{1}{2}$ oz. of sugar in about a quarter pint of boiling water and stir this into the wort. Then bottle the beer using screw-stoppered bottles if you have them. If not use the more readily available crown caps. Put the bottled beer in a warm place for a few days then move it to a cool place for a week or two before using.

Colouring beers is fairly common practice: if your beer is not dark enough, a little caramel may be added.

In all the above recipes use a top fermenting yeast. This is best if it is activated – made into a nucleus as in wine-making. But we cannot use fruit juices for this when making beers. So take a spoonful of malt extract, dissolve this in about half a pint of hot water. Let it cool to about 60° F. (lukewarm) and then stir in the yeast. Do this about two hours before it is needed; the brew will then be in a vigorous state of fermentation quite quickly.

Nineteen

Making Beer
with Grain
Malts

As has been explained, when using grain malts a mashing period is necessary. Different beers need to be mashed at slightly different temperatures, and these are mentioned in the recipes.

Water Treatment

It is sometimes very beneficial to the finished beer to use what is known as water treatment preparations. These are designed to alter the water slightly to produce the type of water used in commercial brewing for the various types of beer. Before you can do this correctly you must obtain an analysis of your water supply from the local water board, and then make good the deficiencies, or use the ready-prepared water treatment from suppliers who market the required salts for the various beers – light ale treatment, etc. These would of course be added to the water at the start, and in the quantities stated by the supplier.

Adjusting the gravity

The same directions as given in the section on making beers from malt extracts apply here – and be sure not to start with a gravity that will make your beer stronger than it should be. Do bear in mind that a little more alcohol will be made after priming (adding sugar to give the necessary effervescence into the beer).

Bitter

4 lb. cracked pale malted barley, 2 oz. crystal malt, 4 oz. medium dark or dark malt extract, dried, $2\frac{1}{2}$ oz. hops (Goldinys if you have them), top fermenting yeast, water as in method on page 128. Mash at 155° F.

Dark Brown Beer (Mild Beer)

$3\frac{1}{2}$ lb. cracked pale malted barley, 6 oz. dark dried malt extract, 3 oz. crystal malt, 2 oz. hops, top fermenting yeast, water as in method on page 128. Mash at 150° F.

Brown Ale

6 oz. crystal malt, $2\frac{1}{2}$ lb. cracked pale malted barley, 6 oz. dark dried malt extract, 2 oz. hops, top fermenting yeast, water as in method on page 128. Mash at 150° F.

Pale Ale (Light Ale)

3 lb. cracked pale malted barley, 3 oz. crystal malt, 2 oz. flaked maize, 2 oz. hops, top fermenting yeast, water as in method on page 128. Mash at 150° F.

Stout

12 oz. patent black malt, 2 lb. cracked pale malt, 12 oz. crystal malt, $1\frac{1}{2}$ oz. hops, $\frac{1}{4}$ level 5 ml. spoonful citric acid, level dessert spoonful black (green) treacle, good beer yeast. Water as in method on page 128. Mash at 148–150° F.

Lager

2 lb. cracked pale malt, $1\frac{1}{2}$ oz. hops, 1 lb. crystal malt, $\frac{1}{4}$ level 5 ml. spoonful citric acid, top fermenting lager yeast. Water as in method on page 128. Mash at 150° F.

Method for Making Beers from Grain Malts

Bring one-and-a-half gallons of water up to about 170° F.
Add the ingredients except the yeast and hops, add a pinch of
salt and stir thoroughly to disperse the ingredients. Allow the
temperature to reach that given in the recipe – reheating
slightly if necessary. Maintain the temperature as given
for one hour. This will most likely be long enough to convert
the starches, but to be on the safe side you can take a small
sample and add a few drops of tincture of iodine. If the sample
turns blue a little longer mashing is necessary.

When mashing is complete, strain the wort through a fine
sieve or three or four thicknesses of muslin. Wash the spent
grains with two pints of very hot water and allow to drain.
Return the wort to the boiling vessel, stir in the hops and boil
vigorously for an hour. Strain again, and squeeze the hops.

Having done this, pour the wort into the fermenting vessel
and make up the two gallons with boiled water that has
cooled. The temperature should now be at about 60° F. If
it is not, raise to this temperature, or allow to cool as necessary.
Take the gravity with the hydrometer and adjust to the figure
required as recommended for malt extract beers, being careful
not to raise the gravity too high. Make sure the sugar is
dissolved and then add the yeast and ferment at as near 60° F.
as you can. After twelve hours, skim off the yeast head, wipe
the fermenting vessel where the scum has stuck to the edges,
give a thorough stirring, cover well and ferment until fermentation begins to slows down. Then skim off any yeast present,
and pour very carefully into gallon jars, fit a fermentation
lock to each and then leave in the warm until fermentation
has ceased.

Having done this, siphon the beer into the fermenting
vessel and prime the bulk using $2\frac{1}{4}$ oz. of sugar to each gallon.
You can heat a small amount of water and dissolve the sugar
in this (about a quarter pint) and stir this into the beer. Then
bottle using screw-stoppered bottles if you have them. If not
use crown caps on pint or half-pint bottles. Keep the bottled
beer in the warm for a week and then in a cool place for
about a month before using.

Twenty

Your Questions Answered

If there were a million books on wine- and beer-making, there would still be questions from people who have read all of them. This is because no matter how detailed a book might be, there are always local conditions, problems peculiar to a certain hobbyist, or the law of maximum cussedness which makes it necessary for certain people to have problems other chaps never have. Nobody can help having problems or points they want cleared up. Beer- and wine-making could be likened to two people buying the same make of car which has come from the same assembly line. One of them will have months of trouble-free motoring while the next will have his car konk out before he reaches the end of the first mile.

The questions and answers here are a cross-section of those received from readers of my other books and of articles of mine which have appeared in many magazines. I do not pretend to answer all your problems – nobody could do that – but I have done my best to help you.

Q: I have been using your recipes and methods for over twenty years and I must confess with much satisfaction – having won several prizes at various shows. But what puzzles me is that you recommend a short second fermentation in the pail before the wine is put into a jar. Is there any special reason for this?

A: There is. When you strain the fermenting pulp and wring it out tightly a lot of minute fruit particles pass through the straining cloth into the still-fermenting wine. During the secondary short period in the pail where the ferment is a little less vigorous than the first, many of these fruit particles settle out to form less or deposit in the bottom of the pail and these can be left behind when putting the wine into a jar. If it were not for this short secondary period in the pail, all this waste matter would go into the jar. This would not be good practice owing to the possibility of it giving 'off' flavours into the wine during the long fermentation in the jar.

Q: Would you let me have your opinion as to whether it is worthwhile trying to keep yeast for any length of time. I have stored yeast in dry airy places, in the fridge, in my fermentation cupboard and I never seem to get such good results with my wines as I do with fresh supplies.

A: You did not say what length of time you have in mind. Normally good-quality dried yeasts will keep well for three or four months if kept in dry, cool, airy conditions, but I would not keep them longer than this.

Q: I have a number of solid rubber bungs – not the sort with holes in for fermentation locks. Would these be suitable for pushing home when putting wine into store?

A: No. But only because they take such a grip on the inside of the jar when left for a long time. If for some reason your wine started to ferment again, the bungs may have taken such a grip that they would not blow out as an ordinary bung would do and the risk is that of exploding jars.

Q: I am nearly seventy, and deaf, but with my hearing aid I manage to understand most of what goes on and the talks that take place at our wine-making circle. Many of my friends and I have several of your books and what puzzles us is that your name is not on the list of speakers who visit wine-making clubs. We are sure that with your wide experience you would have so much to say that would be of interest to all concerned. Would it be too personal to ask why you do not visit clubs to talk to members?

A: I have been expecting this and since you have asked I will tell you. But first let me say that you are very lucky to be able to use a hearing aid. I lost my hearing during the war – June 1940 to be exact – and to such an extent that even today

I can stand within fifty yards of today's mighty jet airliners taking off and not hear a sound. This does not affect my life too much, but obviously I am restricted a little and this is why I never speak in public. But I still wish I could use a hearing aid.

Q: I have just taken the specific gravity of some beer I have made and find that it is down to 1002. Can I suppose that I have made the amount of alcohol I intended to?

A: The specific gravity reading of 1002 that you give means nothing unless you also took the reading before the start of fermentation, for the simple reason that you do not have a figure to compare it with.

Q: I have a recipe for marrow rum which calls for scooping the pips from the marrow and stuffing the cavity with brown sugar. A friend tells me that the recipe will not make marrow rum. Would you advise me please.

A: Your friend is right. All that can happen is that the fleshy part of the marrow and the sugar will slowly dissolve each other to produce an over-sickly sweet syrup.

Q: In your magazine articles and books you always recommend filling the jar to where the neck begins before fitting the lock. I do this of course but, when a little space is left later on when more of the sugar is used up, should I top up again?

A: No. You will notice that I do not include in the recipes the exact amounts of water to use, but in the methods advise you to use so much at various stages. I calculate this taking into account the amount of solids which go into the must as well as the amount of sugar in relation to the type of wine being made – dry, sweet, etc. and plan it so that at the time the wine is put into a jar there is not quite enough to fill it, rather than there being more than will go in. I therefore recommend filling the jar to where the neck begins so that the proper amount of water in relation to the amounts of ingredients and sugar is used. If you top up again at later stages you will dilute the flavour as well as the alcohol content so that more sugar is used up than should be because the yeast will continue to make up the alcohol after you have reduced the amount by adding more water. If your aim was a medium or sweet wine you might, if you repeatedly topped up with water, finish up with a dry wine.

Q: When I put my wines into jars and fit the lock I sometimes find that next day froth from the top of the wine has pushed up into the lock, and on one occasion was actually passing through the lock and running down the outside of the jar. This is obviously caused by a very vigorous ferment and I wonder if you can tell me how to avoid it.

A: As you will have realised, I expect, my directions in the various methods are general-purpose instructions to be followed under normal circumstances and conditions. You will appreciate that no two persons' wines react in exactly the same way, but I cannot take this into account when evolving methods; hence the general-purpose instructions, based on the theory (or hope) that they *will* react in the same way.

Obviously your wines are still fermenting vigorously when put into jars, and in the circumstances it would be wise for you to take careful note by looking at the surface just how vigorously your wines are fermenting when they are due to be put into a jar. You can then decide for yourself whether to leave them in the fermenting pail for a few more days to allow for the vigorous fermentation to die down a little. If you have this trouble again, remove the lock, plug the neck of the jar with cotton wool for a couple of days and then re-fit the lock.

Q: I have been making wines for years using about an ounce of baker's yeast to the gallon. I am now using dried wine yeast with much better results. When I buy these the packet contains enough for up to five gallons. Must I try to apportion the exact amount needed for a one-gallon or a two-gallon lot?

A: No. This is not necessary and if the yeast is not too expensive you can use as much of the packet as you like. It is never wise to use too little yeast. Indeed, it is better to use rather more than is generally advised. It cannot do any harm, but will merely increase the rate of alcohol production and speed fermentation to its conclusion.

Q: Sometimes when I put my wine into jars the solution starts its see-saw motion with bubbles passing through at once and quite rapidly. But at other times it is not until the next day that this happens. Further, sometimes just after I have put wine into a jar and fitted the lock I find the solution drawn up on the ingoing (wrong) side of the lock. Being new to this hobby, I would like your explanation for what appear to me to be oddities.

A: If your wine happens to be fermenting vigorously at the time it is put into jars the lock is likely to start its performance right away. On the other hand if fermentation has slowed a lot when the wine is put into a jar, some time will elapse before bubbles are seen to pass through. The reason the solution in the lock is seen to be drawn up on the wrong side is that quite often fermenting wine is warm through yeast action – yeast generates warmth for itself during early fermentation. It could be that this warmth drives out the small amount of air in the neck of the jar so that when the lock is fitted air is drawn in to balance with the outside atmosphere. Another reason for this happening is when the wine becomes cold. This causes contraction (shrinkage) of the volume of wine, leaving a small space which must be filled with air. If shrinkage is great, then air will be drawn in and the lock will work in reverse. If it is not great, the solution will merely be seen drawn up on the wrong side until enough gas has been produced by the yeast to make the lock work in the proper manner.

Q: I have some old recipes which advise dropping a few raisins into each bottle and leaving them there until fermentation ceases. During this time the corks must be left loosely in the tops of the bottles. In neither of the two books of yours I have do you recommend this. Would you say that adding raisins in this way is a good idea?

A: As you have other books of mine you will know how wrong it is to leave the corks in loosely for any length of time.

As for feeding with raisins; this used to be common practice, but we now know more about wine-making and we know that raisins, or for that matter any particles of fruit, left in the wine for long periods tend to produce 'off' flavours. So there you are. As you have modern recipes and methods to hand I would advise you to use them and forget all about the methods of the past.

Q: In order to let out the air between the wine and the cork as I push the corks home, I insert a piece of string into the top of the bottle and as the cork goes in I pull out the string so that the air can escape. But this always leaves a dirty cloud in the top inch of the wine even though I use new string. How can this be avoided?

A: Quite simply by not using string. I cannot understand why anybody could bother with this idea. If the bottles are filled to one-third up the neck the cork will go in easily. The fact that the small amount of air is compressed does not matter in the least.

Q: When opening my bottled beers I usually get a fountain of froth to such an extent that I lose nearly a third of a bottle of beer. Yet sometimes this does not happen and I pour the beer in the normal way and get a good head on it. Can you tell me what could be the cause of the excess frothing.

A: The reason for so much froth could be that you bottle your beer a day too soon so that there is rather too much fermentation in the bottle or it could be that your storage area is not cool enough or subject to too much variation in temperature. The latter could cause warmth to expand the beer thereby causing compression within the bottle. Cold on the other hand would not have this effect, leaving the beer cool so that it pours naturally. As there are now pressure barrels, bottling beers is not so common.

Q: There seems to be some argument as to whether top or bottom fermenting yeast gives the best results. Can you tell me which is the best to use?

A: Normally, top fermenting yeasts are used for all beers except the lager types. So it is that the top fermenting yeasts are best for one sort and the bottom fermenting for another.

Q: In a price list recently received there were three types of hops offered: Northern Brewer, Fuggles and Kent Goldings. How am I to know which is the best to use?

A: You will only know which is the best to use through trial and error. Some operators swear by one sort while others swear by another. It would not be right for anybody to dictate to you which is precisely the best to use. It depends upon which type of beer you are making and exactly how you want that beer. But do bear in mind that hops play only one part in beer-making. Much depends on other ingredients – even the water, for example – as to what the end product will be like.

Q: How can I evolve beer-making recipes in the hope of turning out good beers while, at the same time, making them different to any at present on the market?

A: First of all, if you decide to make beers nothing like those at present enjoyed by most people up and down the country, how do you know that you will like them? Look at it this way. Recently there came on to the market a product or two which were blends of wine and whisky, or wine and brandy. Naturally, these were quite out of the ordinary and in my opinion a ruination of the wine and waste of the whisky and brandy. I try most new ideas and one in particular struck me as being rather like an experiment I carried out years ago – it was like dandelion wine with a hint of whisky flavour about it. I drank half the bottle and poured the rest away.

The same could be the results of your idea. Bear in mind that it is not just a matter of blending ingredients. Water is the main consideration when deviating from the ordinary. You would have to have a detailed analysis of your water supply made, then take into consideration its acidity or alkalinity, and then adjust it according to whether you are using malt extracts, grain malts, light extracts or dark extracts. Each require a differing chemical make-up of the

water. Some malts will bring about the necessary adjustment
to a certain extent, but others will not. The correct balance
of mineral salts in the water is of utmost importance if you
are to obtain what you think you are aiming at. The only
way you can hope to do what you want is to make as many
beers of the usual type as you can and then experiment. But
do not expect good results until you have studied the chemical
reaction of the ingredients in the mash and the process of
brewing.

Q: Can you tell me whether I get more malt per gallon using
grain malts or malt extracts?

A: If you mean, can you obtain the same amount of malt
from one pound of extract and one pound of grain malt in
one gallon of must, then the answer is – yes, or at least you
should be able to. But to obtain the absolute maximum yield
from grain malts the sparging operation must be almost
perfect. Sparging is spraying the near spent grains with a
finest possible spray to wash off all traces of malt adhering
to the grains. In the brewery this is done with a hot spray
which is hardly more than a fine mist. It therefore washes the
grain without producing too much liquid. On the whole, you
should be able to obtain a specific gravity of 28°, which is a
very good yield.

Twenty-one

A Special Word
for my American
and Canadian
Readers

Because my books sell in enormous numbers in your countries it is only fair that I have a special word or two for you.

You will see that all my recipes are for one-gallon lots. This is because most beginners in this country like to make small lots to start with – just to get the feel of things. But from many letters I receive from your part of the world it is clear that you would not be bothered with such trifling amounts. Indeed, I understand that you make twenty- to thirty-gallon lots and even bigger ones than that and make dozens of lots a year. But you have not yet told me what you do with it all!

If you propose to make a five-gallon lot using one of the recipes in this book, use four times the amounts of all ingredients listed and use five American gallons of water. If you want to make ten gallons then use eight times the amounts of ingredients and ten American gallons of water.

In your country as over here, there are now many suppliers waiting to mail you all your needs – yeast, nutrients, hydrometers, indeed, everything you might require. You will be surprised to find that there are many special wine bases prepared from the fruits from various parts of your country. These are prepared in the same way as concentrated grape juices and the range is very wide – including blackberry, apricot, cherry, gooseberry, purple plum and many others. It would, I am sure, be worthwhile finding out more about these and to use them as I have suggested in various recipes

137

in this book, though of course, the canned variety used in this country might be a little different to yours. Obviously, your best plan is to get in touch with a dealer who will advise you both on this aspect and on the variations in the ingredients for home-brewing. He will advise you as to the best alternative ingredients to use. A list of suppliers in your country appears at the end of this book.

Because huckleberries do not normally grow here in Britain I did not include a recipe for this wine earlier in the book, but to make it you should simply follow the recipes and method for blackberry wines.

If you use sultanas as in many of the recipes in this book you will have to ask for white raisins in your country.

With best wishes to all of my readers throughout the world.

Comparison of Percentage of Alcohol by Volume and Degrees of Proof

The term 'proof spirit' is an antiquated description of the alcohol content of wines and spirits. Actually, the proof spirit content is most misleading because it gives the impression to the average person that a spirit of 75° means that it contains 75 parts per 100 parts (75 per cent) pure alcohol, whereas it does not. Gin for example with a proof spirit content of 70° actually contains 40 parts per 100 of pure alcohol or, in other words, 40 per cent of alcohol by volume. Measuring the alcohol content as by volume is by far the most accurate means.

Alcohol by volume per cent means that if a wine is 15 per cent of alcohol by volume, 15 parts of each 100 is pure alcohol. In other words, if you were to divide whatever amount of wine you might have into 100 parts and the alcohol could be separated, 15 parts of the 100 would be pure alcohol. The 40 per cent by volume gin just mentioned would produce 40 parts of each 100 as pure alcohol. It will be seen from this that per cent proof is quite misleading.

However, most of you will want to know how your alcohol by volume compares with proof spirit and the table below will show you the range wide enough to cover the various degrees of alcohol content that you may be producing in your wines.

Alcohol by Volume per cent	Degrees Proof Spirit
8	13·9
9	15·6
10	17·4
11	19·3
12	21·6
13	22·7
14	24·5
15	26·2
16	28·0

APPENDIX II

Comparison Table of Degrees Fahrenheit and Centigrade

It will be seen that certain temperatures are mentioned in various parts of this book and that these are given as F. = Fahrenheit. But as we are now changing to C. = Centigrade, this comparison table will be found useful. This is not a complete table but covers sufficiently the range of figures you are likely to come across when making wine and beer.

F.	Represents	C.
71·6		22
69·8		21
68·0		20
66·2		19
64·4		18
62·6		17
60.8		16
59·0		15
57·2		14
55·4		13
53·6		12
51·8		11
50·0		10
48·2		9
46·4		8
44·6		7
42·8		6
41·0		5
39·2		4
37·4		3
35·6		2
33·8		1
32·0		0 Freezing

APPENDIX III

Suppliers

England

BREWERS, 97 Dartmouth Road, Forest Hill, London SE23.

BREWING SUPPLIES LTD, 48 Heaviley Road, Stockport, Ches.

CIMBRIA HOME BREWS, Brampton, Cumberland.

CONTINENTAL WINE EXPERTS, Cawston, Norfolk, NOR 75X.

DERMAR HOME BREW SUPPLIES, 11 Crown Street, St Ives, Hunts.

FERMENTA, 58-60 Kingston Road, New Malden, Surrey.

D. F. GREEN, 135 Lynchford Road, Farnborough, Hants.

HIDALGO, 81 Ledbury Road, London W11.

HOME BREW SPECIALISTS, Roundhay Road, Leeds 8.

THE HOME BREWER, 19 Desborough Avenue, High Wycombe, Bucks.

HOME BREWING CENTRE, 120 Pinner Road, Harrow, Middx.

W. R. LOFTUS LTD, 1-3 Charlotte Street, London W1. (No mail order.)

W. R. LOFTUS LTD, Rock Road Store, Torquay, Devon.

W. R. LOFTUS LTD, 1 Okehampton Street, Exeter, Devon.

REGENCY CHATEAU, 255 Grimsby Road, Cleethorpes, Lincs.

ROGERS (MEAD) LTD, 27, Vicarage Road, Wednesfield, Staffs.

SEMPLEX, Old Hall Works, Stuart Road, Higher Tranmere, Birkenhead, Ches.

SOLVINO LTD, 678 High Road, Finchley, London N12 9PT.

VIKING BREWS, Clive Street, North Shields, Northumberland.

VINA LTD, St Johns Road, Waterloo, Liverpool 22.

VINOPAK, 29 Edburton Avenue, Brighton, Sussex, BN1 6EJ.

WINE WORLD OF HUYTON, 21 Sherbourne Square, Huyton, Lancs.

WINECRAFT, Slate Street, Leicester, LE2 0JP.

WINEMAKERS VINEYARD, 96 Brigstock Road, Thornton Heath, Surrey.

CORKS ONLY:
BEECH BROTHERS, Exeter, Devon.
RANKIN BROTHERS, 139 Bermondsy Street, London SE1.

Northern Ireland

ERWIN EXPORTS SERVICES (NI), 217 Shore Road, Belfast 15,
Northern Ireland.

Wales

HOME BREWING AND WINE SUPPLIES, 69 Whitchurch Road,
Cardiff, CF4 3JP.

Scotland

THE BACHONAL, 14 Newton Street, Greenock.

Eire

QUALITY HOME BREWS, 79 Braemor Road, Churchtown,
Dublin 14.

Nearly all of the above will send your requirements by post.

Overseas Suppliers

AETNA BOTTLE CO. LTD, 708 Rainier Avenue South, Seattle 44,
Washington, USA.
WINE SUPPLIES, Box 30230-U, Cincinnati, 0, 45230, USA.
BACCHANALIA, 273 H-Riverside Avenue, Westport, Connecticut
06880, USA.
WINE ART, PO Box 2701, Vancouver 3, B.C., Canada, with
franchises throughout Canada and in most states of
America.
BREWERS TRADING CO., PO Box 593, Christchurch, New
Zealand. This firm also serves most of Australia.

Index

Acids, 24, 34-5, 43, 49, 50, 71-2, 109
Alcohol content, 12, 132
  beers, 114, 118-19, 121, 124, 126
  concentrated grape juices, 55
  fortified wines, 45, 46
  maximum tolerance, 23-4, 25, 44
  proof spirit compared to volume of, 139-40
  use of hydrometer for regulating, 38-43
Apple wines, 101-3

Bacteria, 14-15, 23, 30, 36, 115
Bananas, 11, 12-13, 49, 105, 107
Beer-making, 113-28
Blending, 49-52, 135
Body and bouquet, 10-13
Boiling (in beer-making), 114-15, 125, 128
Bottling
  wine, 17-19, 48-9, 133-4
  beer, 116-17, 125, 128, 134
Bottom Fermenting Yeast, 119, 134-5
Brewing vocabulary, 119-21
Bungs *see* Corks and bungs
Burco boiler, 115, 122

Campden fruit preserving tablets, 15, 44-5, 57
Canned fruits and juices, 58-61
Citric acid, 34-5, 109
Clarifying, 36-7, 62, 93-4, 100
Cleansing dirty jars and bottles, 16-17
Colouring (beer), 125

Concentrated grape juice, 40, 43, 55-8, 63-4, 73, 104-5
'Condition' (of beer), 120
Corks and bungs, 17, 18-19, 31-2, 48, 130, 133-4
Cracked (or Crushed) barley, 120
Crown corkers and caps, 117, 118, 125, 128

Dextrius, 120
Diastase, 120
Dried fruits, 12, 49-50
Dried fruit wines, 51, 84-9

Electra Fibre Line heated tray, 29
Esters, 24, 48

Fermentation, 23-37, 131-3
  quickly-made wines, 53-8
  secondary, 13, 129-30
  use of hydrometer, 38-43
  wine spoilage during, 15-17
Fermentation cupboard, 29, 54
Fermentation locks, 7, 30-3, 125, 128, 132, 133
Fermentation vessels, 9, 15, 54, 57, 115-16, 125, 128
Finings, 120
Flavoured meads, 109-10
'Flor', 11
Flower wines, 11-12, 34, 51, 104-7
Fortifying (wine), 13, 45-6
Frothing, 24, 33, 134
Fruit wines, 26, 34, 35, 40-1
  blending, 50
  canned, 58-61
  made by heat-treatment method, 62-70